The REAL Northern News

by

Robbie MacInnis

Pictou, Nova Scotia to Iqaluit, Nunavut

and back

Copyright ©

Author: Robbie MacInnis

Cover photography: Kelly MacInnis

Book layout & cover design: Pollywog Desktop Designs

Published by Seacroft

ISBN 978-0-9687092-7-6

3

Dedication

To my wonderful family

Kelly, Zachary and Aaron

Table of Contents

Introduction 7
From Pictou to Iqaluit, Nunavut 9
Fast Food or Fast Cash? 11
Language and Education 13
Arctic Char 15
Canada Day Parade 17
Eskimos and Ice cubes 19
The Quickie Mart 21
I Don't Really Hate It 23
Registering En Masse 25
Yukon Jon 27
Quebec City 29
The Bus Tour 31
The Iqaluit Lottery 33
Mall on the Sea 35
Common Sense Transportation 37
The 'Deaths' 39
Northern Lights 41
Junk Food 43
The Two Months of Christmas 45
The Arctic Legion 47
Tough Guy 49
A Spot of Tea 51
Christmas in a Foreign Land 53
The Barter System 55
Red Light District of Iqaluit 57
Sense and Sensibility 59
Rechargeable Batteries 61
Abraham "Abe" Okpik 63
Politics of Sorts 65
Unspoken Brotherhood 67
Alcan and the RCMP 69
The Greenland Stand-Off 71
Oh Where, Oh Where Have my Numbers Gone 73

The Piles 75
Eskimo Pies 77
Nunavut Snow Challenge 79
New Job 81
Tartan Day 83
The Playoffs 85
Toonik Tyme 87
Astro Hill Complex 89
To My Friend 91
Potholes and Mud-puddles 93
Down Home Concert .95
Hiking Day 97
For Sale 99
Mush, Mush! 101
Mush, Mush! - Part 2 103
Polar Man 105
A BumbleBee 107
Carnival 109
Auction 111
The Price of Business 113
Pangnirtung or Panniqtuuq? 115
Inukshuks and Lighthouses 117
Operation Narwhal 119
The Last Straw 121
What Does That Mean, Really? 123
Cape Dorset Carvings 125
The Terry Fox Run 127
Silent Givers 129
Technology 131
Thanksgiving Day 133
Bad Service or No Service 135
Traffic Jams Northern Style 137
Circle Check 139
Passwords, Friends or Foe 141
The DEW Line 143
Christmas Vacations .145

Travel 147
Holiday Stress 149
Santa Claus 151
Happy New Year 153
Brains and Trains 155
The Apprentice 157
The $500 Snowmobile 159
Was it Really The Team or Not? .161
The Return of the Sun 163
Just Doesn't Make Sense, Really it Doesn't 165
A Whole New World 167
The Qulliq 169
How to Live Longer 171
Winter Driving 173
Vegas Vacation 175
Skijoring 177
Soundtracks 179
The Visit 181
Crime and Punishment 183
Earth Day 185
Barbara-Ann of Tumbledown Mountain 187
The Plan 189
Community Games 191
Recycling Reality 193
From Iqaluit to Pictou 195
The Final Chapter 197

Introduction

I have often been asked what got me started writing the Real Northern News. To be completely honest I was facing a new chapter in my life and with every new chapter I have always believed should be new challenges to face.

Life, in the grand scheme of things, is short. To go through it only to do the same thing over and over never seemed quite right to me. Don't get me wrong, I know a lot of great, wonderful people who do just that and are completely fulfilled. They graduated from university, entered the workforce in a particular career and retired from that career roughly a score and a half year later. They raised great families, amassed a modest wealth and are living quite comfortably into retirement.

A part of me envies that stability, but a bigger part of me always gets bored and craves new and greater challenges. I have had an amazing life up until now, one that I wouldn't trade for anyone. I started working as a paperboy for the Cape Breton Post when I was around 10, went on to work a great many, and I mean many, different jobs until I got to where I am now as an account manager for the Royal Bank of Canada. No particular order of jobs. Whenever an opportunity presented itself, I would grab it.

Just a couple of weeks after my marriage in the spring of 2003, we moved lock, stock and barrel into the Canadian Arctic to spend two exciting years. Coming from life in Cape Breton and then mainland Nova Scotia, Baffin Island was a total culture shock. Many of our friends and family insisted that we keep in close touch to let them know how we're making out. What better way than to write a weekly article in the local Pictou County newspaper chronicling our adventures for two years to do just that.

The basic premise behind each column is to show the similarities of our two cultures while still drawing out the differences. It is kind of a way to help people appreciate how wonderful the lifestyle in Pictou County is. People tend to forget the positives and focus mainly on the negatives of living in small N.S. communities. This was a great opportunity to showcase the positives.

Living in an Inuit society and culture was extremely interesting, challenging and most of all, rewarding. At the time we lived in Iqaluit, the population was estimated to be around 60% Inuit with the remainder being from mainly the Atlantic Provinces and Quebec. There wasn't a day that went by that I wouldn't say hello in Inuktitut, French, English, and Gaelic. (The Gaelic was only to one person, Glenn Craig, the local DJ from the radio station. He knew about as much as me, but it was still fun greeting each other in public and talking about the weather in our "Secret language".)

Regardless of all that, it was great being able to share our times living in Nunavut with everyone on a weekly basis. For those who missed out, here you are......

From Pictou to Iqaluit, Nunavut

Life is really an adventure; it throws curves at you and choices that bring out the best or worst in people. For the last several years my boss tried, unsuccessfully, to get me to travel to Labrador City for a weekend workshop. My argument was always the same. If the weather is cold and miserable in Pictou in February, it had to be worse in Lab. City. Low and behold I'm living in Iqaluit, Nunavut now with my new bride. Ah life, what little surprises do you hold in store next?

The first surprise was the airline service; it was, to me at least, super. There were no headphones connected to a radio service, no movies, just like years ago when I first started flying. I had time to relax, read, and think about what's in store for the future. The in-flight service was also great. Starting out with hot towels, then a choice of traditional northern cuisine or a more contemporary meal, followed by a coffee and Baileys (WHEE) topped with whipped cream. All served at a reasonable cost of free.

We decided to grab a taxi from the airport, being laden with two cats and a pile of luggage. The taxis up here operate on a different philosophy than in Pictou, charging a $4.50 flat rate to anywhere in the (ha ha ha) city. Now bear in mind that is per person and the taxis operate like a transit bus system. They cram as many people in as possible and as they let them out, feel free to load in another. So in essence, during a typical ride from the airport to our apartment, the driver could take in over $30 in a drive relative to getting picked up at Sobeys and being taken to the post office.

But life is great, I think I will start telling my boss never to send me to Hawaii for a weekend, let that be a lesson to life.

Next issue I will explore and report why the H#$% it

cost $12.50 for a 6" sub at Subway, and why Toonie Tuesday doesn't apply to KFC up here, plus why I have proof the Leafs will win the cup soon.

Fast Food or Fast Cash?

I think I have solved the question that was vexing every-one for the last number of years. How did Jared possibly lose all that weight on a Subway diet, and if he didn't, how could the company get away with the false advertising. Well, my fellow Pictonians, I believe that he truthfully did, he was shipped to the North and forced to pay the extraordinary prices for his meals. A 6" Meatball sub is only a mere $10.59; while a Steak & Cheese will set you back $12.99. Now, truthfully at home, I only frequented the sub shop while under the influence, and have been reported to be a generous tipper, but I would have cracked if a half a sub cost over a 10-spot. They say that it is the cost of shipping that puts the price up; I would like to see this luxury jet that these thinly sliced deli meats are flying.

After deciding that a sub was not to pass through my digestive tract anytime soon, I thought, hey it's Toonie Tuesday, Hooray. Off to KFC. Good ole dirty bird, aside from a mild case of salmonella poisoning years ago, the Col. has never steered me wrong before. TADA!!!!!!! $7.49 for a 2-piece chicken and fries, $8.99 if you want the dinner. I was surprised but thankfully I went to the sub shop first otherwise I would have been shooting off at the Col. instead. My lesson for today was to eat at home, the only thing fast at these restaurants was the cash being made.

Finally before I leave you, I had to get my drivers licence changed over to Nunavut. I was told and assured of the location because every building in Iqaluit is numbered accord-ing to when it was built. So building 2209 could be by the air-port while building 2210 could be on the other side of town. I really pity the pizza delivery guy (not that I could probably afford delivery, let alone the pizza).

I decided to walk there to avoid showing up for my picture with a head of unruly hair from taking my ATV helmet off. (vanity is a disease). So off I trot to the office. After an invigorating hike in the brisk northern air, I arrive at the building labeled Motor Vehicles. But nowhere inside was the actual office, although well marked as being on the first floor, where I was. I decided to ask someone and they told me, smiling "Oh they moved into a government building downtown and really didn't tell anyone." I politely thanked her for her gracious help and left again, this time in rain showers.

After visiting several government buildings and getting the same response, "they are in the Blah Blah Building," I finally reached the door that read in big letters, Dept. of Motor Vehicles, only to find a sign on the glass reading, "Office closed for the afternoon because of computer malfunction." Perfect, just @#^%$$ perfect. It took me almost 2 hours in the cold and rain, only to find a government office closed.

Two things I learned: one, that Government is the same up here as everywhere else, and two, that the Leafs will win the cup in the very near future.

I just walked over the better part of Hell's half acre and Ladies and Gentlemen it was froze over.

Language and Education

I never realized how much I took Pictou County and its landscape for granted until I arrived here and took a little boo around. There were some really glaring differences that took my breath away. It is June and the harbour is still frozen and I just left Pictou, with its yachts, sailboats, and of course the Hector proudly adorning the skyline. (Sniff-sniff) I'm told the icebreaker will soon be here to give us some beach weather.

The Iqaluit skyline also differs in it's apparent lack of trees. As I stroll one of three paved streets (mind you there are a lot more than three streets), I am stunned at all of the wooden buildings, built of wood I assume, but no trees. Can't be, I said to myself, wooden houses built without trees. Are these people some sort of wizards? Of course not, we are well above the tree line, and apparently the bush and dandelion line as well.

This treeless environment brings me to my point of language and education. I studied linguistics and languages the last two years down "south" in Antigonish, at the little University of ST.F.X, and learned that a language needs to be used constantly and passed on to younger generations in order to survive. I was taught that of all the native languages, northern Inuit languages have the best chance of continued survival. This is mainly because of their strong will to survive as a people and culture low these hundreds of years, and the relatively low impact white society has had upon them compared to the other aboriginal groups in Canada.

One striking thing I learned since being here is that educators have developed their own curriculum that educates the students in an environment that is more familiar and accessible. The students are no longer required to know how to spell tree, pig, cow, horse, or any other thing not indigenous to the area. Well done to them. They are strengthening their culture, hence their language, with such a simple device as not teaching their children about objects that they can't associate with personally. Something to think about.

I would love to take these children to the Pictou exhibition and watch their faces. I have taken the animals, the displays, and such for granted for years, complained that each one was not as good as the year before. This year as the Pictou exhibition looms upon you think of us up north, I know I will probably be willing to pay anything to smell the pulp mill coupled with the horse barns again on that day.   AH! The sweet, sweet smell of (sniff-sniff) HOME……

Arctic Char

I had the pleasure of eating at the Navigator Inn Restaurant the other day; I decided to go for the Surf and Turf, which up north is Arctic Char and Caribou steak. The meal was superb; Arctic char belongs to the salmon family and is considered an acclaimed delicacy to gourmets everywhere. They taste like a mild variety of Margaree salmon, and should be tried by anyone who gets the opportunity. The caribou was also a nice treat. It has a pleasant taste that is slightly gamey but not overpowering.

Now that the snow is finally starting to disappear, and the Inuit are getting their snowmobiles off the harbour, talk is all about fishing the great beast called char. I have never professed to be a great fisherman (fisherperson to be politically correct I suppose) but that never stopped Ahab either and look where that got him. So off to the store to get my fishing stuff, then to the license office (expand the truth a bit in order to get a resident license in lieu of a non-resident license) and then to Sylvia Grinnell Park to where the open river is supposed to be.

After arriving at the river and finding it open and raging, I decided to cast my line and reel in my bounty of char. The only possible way I could have sucked worse is if I stood on the shore and threw my entire rod and reel in the river. My line got tangled and knotted on the cast; my only lure and hook snagged on the bottom and broke off in my struggle to reel the big rock in. My big plan of daddy bringing home the supper and being rewarded for my prowess was destroyed on my first and last cast.

The irony of the situation is that my new father-in-law, Ira Grant, spent years working at the fisheries school in Pictou. The fisheries school, and me, his son-in-law, is a fishing idiot. How will I ever live this one down? Hopefully he won't read this article and NOBODY else tells him. Ah well maybe the next time out will redeem me in his eyes....

Canada Day Parade

I never thought that it could be so cold on July 1, but there it was 4 degrees and you could see your breath. Canada Day started with a flea market and pancake breakfast, then a parade, followed by a carnival (indoors of course) and ended with a dance from 6-8pm.

Living with two cats, I figured we had enough fleas, and I don't eat breakfast so the first two activities were out. The parade was supposed to start at 12:30, so we got on our ATV and headed to the parade route. The parade was already enroute when we arrived and we had to make an emergency parade route decision in order to catch "the entire parade". My days of Lobster Carnival parades, Festival of the Tartans, and of course Westville Canada Day parade fresh in my head from previous years, I was expecting the worse and wasn't disappointed.

The Parade consisted of 19 entries, of which nine were emergency vehicles. An Air Cadet Flag Party, two corporate entries, (Mary Browns Fried Chicken's "Chicken Man" and Subway's "Sub Man"- costing approx. $2.5 million in relation to size of the regular subs), Brownies and the Inuit association entries, an RCMP marching contingent, a couple of ATV's with red and white balloons attached following along with the ever popular "Polar Man", Iqaluit's self-proclaimed superhero.

Now I realize all too well that Pictou has its fair share of colorful characters, like little cartoons put on earth for our enjoyment, but this guy takes the cake. He dresses daily in his black toque, white sweatshirt and pants; with a long black vest, topped off with a black eye mask to hide his identity. Rumor has it that he is solely responsible for the elimination of the evil gingivitis, contrary to some popular TV adverts.

The carnival was a delight, there was a free BBQ, a huge variety of games for the children, a community band playing on a platform (I now realize that bad musicians never die, they just come here) but overall there must have been half the, ha ha ha, city's population there. I'm so sorry, I just can't say city in regards to here without laughing.

Overall the day was pretty interesting, and I can't wait to see what the Iqaluit "Fly-Your-Own-Lobster-In" Carnival will be like. A few others and I are going to celebrate the event here. So when you are at the Beer Garden, tip your glass for Kelly and I, as we will for you....

Eskimos and Ice cubes

As a young boy growing up, I always laughed at the notion of a salesman selling a refrigerator to Eskimos in the cartoons. Picture of a well-suited salesman standing outside of the igloo with the fridge plugged in next to it. (HA HA That's Gold Jerry, Gold) As well, people also used to use the phrase, "Oh that so and so is so slick or smooth, he could sell ice cubes to an Eskimo." Well I'm happy, or maybe a little sad, to report that a person could indeed make money up here selling ice cubes to the Inuit, not Eskimos, as I will explain.

I have taken a job at the local Quickie Mart, to keep myself busy until something more substantial comes along. The money is good, don't get me wrong, but the people I work with... oh, don't even get me started. There is ole 'Crackie', Jimmie, the thousand question guy; Steve, and the rest, but that's another story. Back to my point, people are always coming in and asking if we sell ice, which we don't. Apparently nobody does from what I found out. I feel like buying a used ice machine from a hotel, plug it in the hallway of our apartment building, bag the ice and sell it either at the Quickie Mart between my squishie machine and soft serve ice cream machine, ha ha, or door to door.

Now that brings me to the interesting and confusing point of why they are called Inuit versus Eskimo. The ascendancy of Inuit culture, through good reportage and the establishment of Nunavut, has conditioned southerners to say "Inuit" instead of "Eskimo." You see the confusion lies in the fact that there are still Eskimos, but Eskimos are not Inuit, and vice versa.

Now as far as I can ascertain, the Mongol-type peoples of North America began in Alaska and separated into many cultures as their numbers grew and they expanded east. Inuit, which translates as "the living ones who are here" denotes a sense of place, of having arrived, a memory that they knew they had kin elsewhere. Conversely, Alaskans are descendents of people who stayed in the west and as such have their own names for themselves. Inuit is a blanket name for the different cultures in the east, while Eskimo is the blanket term for the west.

The old thinking was that word Eskimo came from Cree, meaning "eaters of raw meat" derogatorily of course. It was also thought that it was overheard by French missionaries, distorted to "Esquimaux" or "Esquimau" then anglicized to "Eskimo". Either way the term Eskimo only stands to remind the Inuit of the days when the missionaries kidnapped them, had flea powder dumped over them and assigned "Eskimo numbers" to them. Not a pleasant time…lessons learned hopefully.

Every year, we celebrate New Scotland Days and show off our Scottish history and culture to the tourists. This year let us all try to reflect a little bit on all of the cultures that surround us everyday and help celebrate what makes Pictou, Pictou County and Canada such a great place to live.

Next time, Life at the Quickie Mart …

The Quickie Mart

One thing everybody does, whether they realize it or not, is feel a great deal of comfort in a routine of stopping at the same places on a regular basis. Some people will have their whole day's rhythm thrown off by not stopping at Tim's at the rotary to get their medium double-double, or people feel like they missed something if they don't go to the post office to get their mail, chat with others and read the community kiosk outside. (A big hello and thank you to the folks at the Pictou Post Office for their help in our move. Look out in two years; it is all coming back plus more, except the bulk cat food. We can't wait.)

The Needs store, East End Grocery, Millside, and the list goes on for meeting places. But up here there is NO Tim Horton's, yes you did hear me correctly, no Tim's. My first reaction was Gwawk!!!! Then a string of expletives that are rated 18. (Oops he he).

The Quickstop where I work, Quickie Mart, as I like to

call it, is the northern equivalent, and it is a comfort to know that some things survive the cultural gaps in society. The same people arrive @ the same time each day, usually buying the same stuff, building an unstated but undeniable relationship between me and them, which develops into an unspoken community within a community. A good thing I believe. I think???

I started out as a regular employee, worked my way up to assistant manager, then manager all in a span of one month. (Yippee, me schoolin' is startin to pay off). As you can imagine the other employees didn't take too kindly to that. Jimmie, Ole Crack Corn (my nickname for him, in private of course, from the rhyme), the only other full time employee, takes every opportunity to challenge and question my authority. He tells me regularly "that's not the Nunavut way" of doing things, and he doesn't even care if he has a valid reason or not. He tells me he is a recovering "everything" and he is really abrupt, rude in my books, about everything. A typical call: The phone rings, "Quickstop" is shouted in the receiver. "Not here" then BANG!!! Ha ha ha I thought Holy Smokes, so I took ole Crackie aside and asked him as nicely as possible if he could answer the business phone more nicely, and his response was "that's not the blah blah way" arghh!!!! Anyway, I finally have him up to shouting "Bye" before the bang. Baby steps, Robbie, baby steps.

The other part time employees, seem to be under the assumption that calling in to work an hour or two late and telling me "that they are GOING to be late" is a perfectly acceptable reason not to be there. I tell them that they are already late and to get to work right away. They laugh thinking I'm funny and eventually arrive. They go out on the land, miss work, don't call in ahead of time, and expect to be treated like royalty when they return.

Now, the Quickstop is to NorthMart like Needs is to Sobeys and they control all the hiring and firing, leaving my hands tied. Usually at this point I release a few endorphins, put a stupid smile on my face and dream about the days when I'll be able to get a large coffee, with just milk, walk into the local Pictou "Quickie Mart" and be treated with the good ole fash-ioned Nova Scotia hospitality I am so missing......

I Don't Really Hate It

I really had a difficult time with last week's column. Every time I read it, I seemed to come across as being hateful, racist and/or bigoted. I must have re-wrote the column a dozen times but I think I got my point across in the end. The point being that I am the one who is outside of my cultural background and that I have to be more understanding of their way of doing things. It made for a real challenge of my leadership abilities, but thankfully I have overcome most of the obstacles (I think).

I reread my other columns and started to see a pattern emerge, a pattern that depicted me hating it here. Which is the main point of this week's column. My first impression of Iqaluit back in the middle of May was that "I didn't hate it" and that I would have a good chance of actually liking it albeit not enough to stay past our expected return date. I think the reason was, that in some strange way, it reminded me of home.

The east coast invasion over the years shows up in very subtle ways and makes each day more bearable. The Legion and other beverage rooms sell Keith's, (or so I'm told), the grocery departments sell quite a number of Purity products, while the DJ for the new radio station (RAVEN ROCK) is Glen Craig, from out by the Mira, bye. His distinctive voice and references to Nova Scotia landmarks often make me forget that I'm north of 60, even if for a brief moment. The pharmacy staff at North Mart are all from NS, and all have ties to Pictou County, Kelly (formally of Fulmore's, hi guys) included of course. There is a noticeable lack of pipe bands up here (I know some people might think that to be a selling point to move here…ha ha) but the fiddle and its distinctive Celtic style is alive and well. The Hudson Bay Company trappers and buyers brought it with them low those 300 some years ago. Today there are music camps and festivals dedicated to maintaining the music. But the best clue is overhearing conversations at the Quickie Mart, or passing on the street; people using terms like "Bootin' her down the road" and "up here on a Pogey run" always make me smile and think of home.

So even though there is a challenge in submerging yourself in a different culture, it is a credit to our proud east coast traditions to be still seen, heard and accepted even if it is subtle. So as much as I do gripe and I will more and more, what with the endless daylight hours, mosquitoes the size of cormorants, and summer days reaching a high of 3 with a wind chill of -1. It does have some redeeming points aside from the previously mentioned. I never once mowed the lawn up here, and I foresee a fall filled with days of not raking leaves. And although I was stuck in a traffic jam twice, it wasn't because of roadwork, so there really is a silver lining. Who would have thunk it…still four months down . (Not that I'm counting)

Registering En Masse

One aspect of moving to a new community is the inevitable fact that you have to, or at least try to, make new, but not necessarily improved, friends. One way of doing this is to get out into the community and engulf oneself in the community groups that are available. Having been transplanted to Pictou from heaven (Cape Breton), information about community groups was spread around mostly by word of mouth and the odd Pictou Recreation newsletter. Was it an effective method? At the time, I thought so, however after seeing how it is done in Iqaluit, it left a little to be desired.

The city (ha ha ha, still makes me laugh) of Iqaluit has one day dedicated to a mass registration for any and all community groups. The groups all meet in the arena and set up tables or booths displaying their respective aims and goals. The day and times that each group meet are well displayed, the cost is readily available along with any other pertinent information needed to make your decision. From a prospective clients point of view, I think this is a brilliant idea. I had the opportunity to see all at once what the community had to offer. Not signing up for one thing and two weeks later finding out that something else, far more interesting was available at the same time. A typical family of four, have the opportunity to set their weekly schedules at the same time, know well in advance what perils and transporting hazards are in store for the next 10 months, and hopefully avoid them. I think that this idea, albeit the "Nunavut way", could easily be adopted at home, maybe not this year but for future years to come. Something for Nicole to think about, at least ponder anyway. On an interesting side note, Pictou's former Recreation Director, Gerard MacIsaac, was one of the first recreation directors here in Iqaluit.

Now before I get back to the Quickie Mart, I'll leave you

with one quick Crackie story. The other weekend I had to pop into the store for something or other, and while I was chit chatting to the employees, in walks Jimmie sporting his Quickie Mart apparel. He smartly walked in behind the till, picked up his partial plate (that he left sitting on the counter in plain view since the day before), threw it in his mouth and was about to leave without saying a word. Now in hindsight, I really should have said nothing but me being a smartass, I asked Ole Jimmie if he liked his work clothes so much that he wore them on his days off. Without even hesitating, Crackie said, "I wore them so that the part-timers would know that I work here and not think I was stealing these teeth." I'm not sure if I laughed in my outside voice or not, but, all the employees know Jimmie. Plus, the thought of a complete stranger coming into the store, eyeballing the set of false teeth and brazenly walking behind the counter, putting them in their mouth and leaving, is prolly one of the funniest notions to pass through my tortured mind in awhile. I looked at Jimmie for a minute, closed my eyes and nodded my head, and said " Uhuh, Good thinking Jimmie, Good thinking Bud."

Next time, camping with Yukon Jon..

Yukon Jon

If you ask any one of my friends (yes, I do have some) if I like to go hiking and camping, the answer would be a big "You betcha". So when my next-door neighbor, Yukon Jon McCotter, invited me to go out on the land for the weekend I jumped at the chance. People are strongly advised against going out on the land alone and/or without a guide because the threat of wolves and polar bears is real and ominous. Yukon John was born and raised in Whitehorse (hence the Yukon), but has undeniable ties to Nova Scotia. He studied at the Coast Guard College in Westmount, and previously worked in Barrington Passage with the Dept. of Fisheries, before transferring to Iqaluit. Yukon Jon is an Eskimo and is very proud of his heritage, although he now calls the Maritimes home due to his stay there. Another credit to our hospitality.

All I had for a rucksack was my ST.F.X. backpack, but I thought it is only 10 km in to the campsite and only for two nights. I purchased a 3 lb fill sleeping bag rated to 0 degrees, thinking that would be sufficient, tied that to my pack and met Yukon at the car. We drove what seemed like 5 minutes up the "Road to Nowhere" pulled off to the shoulder and got out. (It actually took 7 minutes, and that is the actual name of the road for good reason)

As we started to unload the gear, Jon passed me about 60 lbs of wood to carry. I realized then, rather blondly, that we were going to have to carry the firewood into the site. No trees equals no firewood. No problem I thought, what's another 60 lbs of weight attached to my school bag. After all was attached, it was time to set out.

The terrain is nothing like Pictou's. It is a lot of rocks surrounded by a spongy, moss-like vegetation. Great for holding water and hiding uneven ground. First we had to traverse an 8-

10 foot stream, then it was a steady climb of a couple hundred feet. Yukon had to be carrying well over 130 lb, yet he was off like a mountain goat. Not me; I stopped briefly for what seemed like a mild heart attack, then again for another. When he said we still had two more hills like this to climb, I finally faked an injury, Ha ha ha ha. Terrible I know but better than my body exploding like a pumpkin filled with explosives. I never realized how out of shape I had become. We broke camp right there by the lake. After the camp was set, Yukon explained that his ancestors would burn tundra bush during the summer and seal blubber during the winter. But that was then and this is now. Around 11 pm it started to rain, then snow, rain and snow again, I shook and shivered all night. Who would have thought freezing temps and snow in August? On a brighter note, we didn't need to ward off predators. Yukon asked at one point, if a bear should show itself, which I wanted, the bear spray or the axe. I told him "just the car keys, I'll have it all warmed up by the time you get there." (he he). Well it would be all downhill.

Quebec City

The one thing veteran northerners (ex-southerners-not Inuit) will tell anyone moving to the North, is to get out every chance you get. That's the true irony of living here. To survive the North is to leave the North. Now, I was never really a good listener, as a matter of fact there were times I didn't even listen to myself, which never turned out well. I was always more of a selective listener only hearing what I wanted to hear. Regardless of that fact, this was advice I did hear, listen and planned on putting into practice.

Recently as some are aware, I was awarded a medal by the Governor General and had the opportunity to travel to historic Quebec City for the Investiture. This all expense paid trip was provided for us by the GG and paid for by the tax payers of Canada. (Thanks everyone, He he he) Anyway, I had the choice of going to Quebec City in September or Ottawa in February. Hhhhhhhmmmmmm Lets see! I could leave the cold up here and enjoy a beautiful, warm, long weekend in Quebec City, or wait and leave the really, snot-freezing cold here in February to go to the icy cold weather in Ottawa. That decision took all of, oh, 3 nanoseconds to decide. The bonus of September is that Family could travel on good roads and spend the weekend with us. Yayyyyyyy!!!!!!

I won't get into all the details, however a few are noteworthy. The ceremony was flawless, the location breathtaking and the experience extraordinary. I have never had the experience of being in the company of twenty-one strangers and 45 minutes later having shared a part of their lives; a deep, life changing part of their lives. How many times have you flown on a plane with strangers, sat on a bus and looked for someone you knew, or even had a cup of coffee at Tims and "people watched" wondering about them. What circumstances have brought them to the same place as you, at the same time, going the same way, doing the same thing? How could that be without you knowing anything about them? I left the ceremony feeling both humbled by the experience and proud to be Canadian. I also left feeling good about humanity, having shared in the experience of others.

One other big surprise was Kelly's parents, Ira and Barbara Ann Grant; along with Joyce and Danny Talbot were there to cheerlead me. Although I was only allowed one guest, they were all present, and I am not quite sure who Barbara Ann muscled to the mat in order to get in but I was glad they did. After the luncheon, we all went exploring Old Quebec, which lead to the pie incident….next issue.

I would like to extend my deepest thanks to everyone who made this day so special by either nominating me or making me listen to myself that fateful night. I think the residents of Ross Street are truly good neighbors and I am grateful.

The Bus Tour

Last week there was mention of a pie incident in ole Quebec, but first I have to set the scene earlier in the day. Long gone are the days of glancing at my watch and rushing off to the Pictou shopping center to get to the beer store before it closes. In hind-sight I really should have told them I was leaving, they were probably worried when I didn't show up for a couple of days. (You can take down my missing person sign).

Up here in Iqaluit, there is no place to buy alcohol like the NSLC. There are a few bars and the Legion, but other than that, you would have to go through the red governmental tape. First you have to get a liquor permit from the Goverment, then wait three days in order for them to see if you are responsible enough to have booze, then it is flown in from Yellowknife at an extraordinary cost, ($125.00 for 24 Bottles of Keith's!). I know I won't be complaining next trip to the NSLC. In case you are wondering, home brew is being concocted as we speak, thanks to Helen, and I have a back up plan in effect utilizing the sealift.

Back to my point, Saturday in Quebec City started off with us trying to locate the nearest liquor store in order to stock up on "other than beer" alcohol supplies. So the impression we gave the hotel staff was that we, as a family, couldn't start our day without a trip to the SAQ (Quebec's NSLC). A couple of hundred dollars later, five Nova Scotians were sitting on a park bench with bags and bags of booze as people started their day. We did manage to attract quite a few looks especially from the front desk staff. Ha ha! I would love to have heard that conversation after we got on the elevator. The booze wasn't all for us in case you were wondering, we had a list for other people as well, so there!!!

After lunch we all decided we would take the Gray Line bus tour of Old Quebec which sounded like a lovely, non-ener getic way of seeing the historic city. So we all piled in. With the exception of three Chinese men, a rather portly gentleman and his guest, there were very few other people. The Grants decided the back of the bus would be best for us and we set off on the tour. The first stop was at the main bus terminal for some reason or other, but we had a chance to get off for a coffee or snack. Which we did, Ira went on behalf of the bunch of us and came back an impressive bag of treats, but so did the portly man and his was just for himself.

Well the tour driver was soooooooo boring, one Chinese man fell asleep while the other two chatted among themselves, and the rest of us ate because between the roar of the engine and the monotone voice of an over used tour speech, we couldn't really pay attention enough to hear. The next stop was the Petit Champlain. If you ever get the chance you have to try the cheese pie at the "Greasy Pig", it is fantastic. After the twenty-minute shopping stop, we reloaded the bus, a whole pie and utensils in hand, and began the gorging as we drove the rest of the tour. All I can say is Ira was a lucky, lucky man to get by the portly guy unscathed as he entered the bus with the pie and, we were all lucky to squeeze out of the bus, and our pants, after the tour. Ah, what a sight we must have been, touring the majestic, historic old city, considered to be the birth place of Canada by some and all we could concentrate on was pie, good ole fashioned pie. Now after hearing that, you can't tell me we aren't true Nova Scotians. Come on I dare you....

The Iqaluit Lottery

I was never one to really gamble. I buy the odd scratch ticket from time to time. I'll get a 6/49 when the jackpot is high because in my mind that is when everyone else says, "Whoa, this jackpot is getting out of hand," and backs out, hence making my chances inevitably better at winning good money and not chump change like one or two million. Yeah right, but it is true to a certain degree, more people buy as the jackpot goes up. Up here in the North, it is the same but unlike in Pictou County, there is only one place to buy Lotto tickets. One booth in Northmart manned by one person and operated at come-by-chance hours at best. The lottery is Western Lottery and has Plus instead of Tag. Coming from a place where you can gamble anywhere from the gas station to the pool hall (VLT's) I find that the fever is not as strong up here. The Lotto booth is busy some days but there are days when there is nothing. Maybe limiting the availability of buying tickets has the ability of limiting the demand and social issues attached. HHHHmmmm, that's one theory, mine is similar but also takes in the "Iqaluit Lottery" factor as well.

I coined the phrase "Iqaluit Lottery" only because it is here that I took notice of the phenomena. Any cashier in Sobey's, convenience stores, or anywhere else a debit machine is used might know what I am talking about. It is that intense concentration, the crossed fingers and knotted stomach of customers as they wait for the banks to grant them one last payoff. They usually try to act casual but you can see the perspiration starting to form on their forehead, and never do their eyes leave the pin pad waiting for that one glorious word to appear "Approved". When it does you can see the joy in their confident faces, as if they picked the right horse or numbers, the look is also to let me know that they knew all along that they were going to win and we both had nothing to worry about. The opposite is just as you would expect, that look of horror on their faces; the realization of not "winning" their purchases is undeniable. Of course we have to try again because they "might" have entered the wrong pin code, next is the blaming of the banks for making some mistake or other, the odd call to the bank is made if during banking hours, but the end result is always the same. No apology for holding everyone up, no effort made to help put back the products. No doubt they will be back, sometimes the very same day, to prove to everyone they should have been right the first time!

I could never be accused of being a financial wizard but I always know what my balance is in my account. In some way I think they do as well, but the thrill of the Iqaluit lottery (trying to get as close to zero without going over because lord knows we can't carry a balance over) keeps them entertained without really gambling. Life is great ain't it……

Mall on the Sea

One of the first things I noticed driving through Iqaluit when I arrived was what I thought was a plethora (big word of the week means "a lot" he he!) of large dumpsters. Behind most apartment buildings and homes were these huge commercial dumpsters. I thought this was rather odd until someone told me the difference. Maybe it's a testament to my stupidity but it turns out, these are Iqaluit two-car garages - make that two-skidoo garages. They are not dumpsters but old cargo containers off the sealift ships that make their way to Baffin Island every year. I think this is a very inventive way of "recycling" these discarded hunks of metal.

This brings me to my topic this week - the SeaLifts themselves. Iqaluit is a small town built around the water much like Pictou. At home on Pier C, pulp boats come and go along with the odd Coast Guard vessel. Unless you're directly involved in the shipping industry (no comments please Dave Fulmore), the business conducted on Pictou's waterfront can easily go unnoticed. Here in Iqaluit, the Bay and the boats that come and go from it, are a lifeline. Many companies specialize in sealift deliveries and will arrange anything from a year's supply of Pepsi, or bulk products from a huge catalogue of groceries, to a new family car. Without the seaLift boats, the only option for residents is to ship things airfreight which is extremely expensive.

Much talk is focused around the sealifts. "Will we make the seaLift?" "Is the next sealift in yet?" "Are you going to work this seaLift?" When word arrives that a ship is one or two days out from harbour, the sign up sheets go up. Companies are desperate to get enough able bodies to unload the boats in a timely fashion. Kids as young as twelve (the legal working age in Nunavut!) can earn $12.00 an hour for a few days work. Sure beats a paper route!

The boats arrive every two to four weeks beginning the end of June and ending when the ice in Hudson Bay becomes

too difficult to navigate (any day now as I write this in the middle of October). Today as I look out my window, people out on the bay are scurrying like little ants to unload the latest, if not last, boat of the season. This floating "Costco" (or "Price Club" for us old timers) delivers many treasures for the population of Iqaluit before heading up Island to northern communities. For myself and a group of co-workers, it (hopefully!) contains an entire winter's ration of beer. God love the Molson company in Montreal. By ordering in bulk we will end up paying little more than it would cost you to run to the NSLC for a 24 of beer. We've been waiting all summer for this particular boat. I'm getting a little misty eyed just thinking about it. I think I'd better sign off and head downtown to check on our libations. Santa's come early for Robbie this year!!

Common Sense Transportation

Anyone standing on the corner by Ahead of Hair would be able to tell you exactly what passed them by in the last hour without even looking half the time, passenger cars, pickup

trucks, SUV's, and even the odd transfer truck. But in the north you have to be a little more observant. The bylaws permit ATV's and snowmobiles to share the road with the rest. Now I know what you are going to say "Robbie, what madness! The world is going to hell in a hand basket..... hell in a hand basket I says". I thought the same thing at first, however it makes perfect sense to me now, at least for up here.

The roads are all unpaved with the exception of three. Snow is a reality, and living off of the land is an unquestionable part of the society and culture. By all accounts driving an ATV during the spring, summer, and fall, and/or your snowmobile fall, winter, and spring seems logical. All the usual road rules apply and are enforced, and everybody respects each other on the road. Since arriving, we purchased our own ATV and have enjoyed every minute touring the town, oops sorry "city", and countryside. You have to keep in mind that speed limits on the roads never exceed 40 km/hr. Most being 30 km/hr, which considering the road conditions is quite fast enough. When we make our triumphant return home, we are really going to miss the ability to jump on the bike to run errands.

Speaking earlier of Ahead of Hair, I want to say hi to Linda and the rest of the folks, I really miss you. Since up here, I have come to the realization that my hairdresser has no training whatsoever, and feels no remorse in charging me a cool $30.00 to cut what is left of my hair. Yeah and apparently that's legal. Go figure.

Finally, I feel compelled to discuss Ole Crackies business aspirations. Jimmie told me that he plans on going to the metal dumpsite and bringing home discarded washers and dryers. He plans on rebuilding them and selling them for half the retail price. Which on face value is not really a bad plan, so I asked Crackie if he knew anything about repairing washers or dryers, to which he replied that he didn't. He said that he was planning on taking his own washer and dryer apart, comparing it to the ones that are broken and replace what was missing. Ha ha ha ha Where would I start. After this happened, I realized that the difference between a twenty minute conversation with him and eternity is very little.

The 'Deaths'

Looking back at my youth and growing up in Cape Breton, I can remember some things with exceptional clarity while other things tend to blur. The Post is one thing I remember. My father would read every inch of the paper, cover to cover and if there was time read parts again. The paper was different then, it was delivered after school in lieu of the morning, and was read after supper was finished. My Mother (hi mom) on the other hand would take the paper first and check the "deaths." It wouldn't really matter if she read anything else. As a matter of fact, she usually wouldn't look for the paper until the next day. I used to think it a weird practice, but since we've moved and have the Advocate and Cape Breton Post delivered weekly, I find myself checking the deaths first and then reading the remainder. I am finally at that age (18 with experience is all you get) when I need to know who be and who not be, so to speak.

In Iqaluit, there are two local rags, The News North and Nunatsiaq News (pronounced Nun-at-si-aq) Nunatsiaq is truly local being from Iqaluit, while the News North is a division of Northern news services out of Yellowknife with an office in Iqaluit. Both cover the local news in both languages and seem to do an equal job of covering local issues. One thing missing in both papers however is a lil section called the obituaries. Since I've been here I have probably heard, read or seen about a dozen tragic deaths but nothing about the graceful passing of others. There is the odd memoriam posted in each, an article here or there about how one is missed from an organization after passing on but no formal obituary. And no one cares, that's what I found odd.

I have found that the communities are so close knit that there is no real demand for the section. Usually within 12 hours of a passing, the community as a whole is in the know. They take it upon themselves to spread the word. As far as the per-sons' life story told in a paragraph or two they already know what it would read. I was working last Sunday morning and a customer came in and told me about the passing of John Doe. The look on my face told him enough to explain that he was the one who drove the sewer truck, red hair, smoked Players smooth. Ah, nodding my head in acknowledgement, what hap-pened? The rest is unimportant but explains how the deaths are announced in the North. I've only been here 5+ months and am included in the information highway (or information dirt road in this case)

It makes me ponder at how I would be explained; The Quickie Mart employee who came from Cape Breton via Pictou, who was so good looking that he was considered the Tom Cruise of the Arctic………..it makes one think. It really does…

Northern Lights

I was watching ASN last week, the last resort for TV watching in Pictou, but a news lifeline for Maritimer's here in the north. A day without Couch Potato, Steve Murphy would be insufferable, what, with all the playful banter between him and Peter Coade. Ha ha ha, good times. Anyway they were discussing the phenomenon called Aurora Borealis, the "Northern Lights" and how brilliant they were in Nova Scotia. They were also explaining how they could be seen as far away as Florida. Wow, Florida, what a spectacular event. Now if you were saying to yourself, "If we had such a great show, picture what they had in Iqaluit." Well I'm here to say, rather sadly, I didn't bother to get up off the couch to have a gander out the window. Might explain why my pants are shrinking at an alarming rate. Hmmmmm, food for thought. Mmmm Food. In my defense, I do have a reason, albeit a stupid, grasping-at-straws reason in order to justify my missing the wonders of the celestial skies that evening.

We made the move from Pictou to Iqaluit in June, and during June it only gets dark for about three hours a night here. From about 1:00 am to about 4:00 am, then it is bright again. So I never really had the opportunity to see the lights. Since June, we experienced even shorter nights, eventually seeing up to 24 hours of daylight, making stargazing impossible even for the most avid watcher. (Yeah, yeah, yeah, I also realize, 24 hours to fish the Mighty Beast called Artic Char and I still couldn't catch one, what a dummy I am, blah, blah, blah). However, now the sun rises at 7:30 am and it is pitch dark at 3:30 pm. This will inevitably lead up to the opposite-24 hours of darkness. Darker days now upon us, also mean colder days. The ground has been snow covered for 4 weeks, and the weather has been hovering at -10, with a wind chill of -25 on average the last 10 days. That doesn't really add up to fun times outside for me. Not when I have a perfectly good couch, a big bag of potato chips, with dip of course, and a wonderful evening of prime time entertainment on ASN. Can't miss Night Side at 11:00 pm, followed by Seinfeld. I figure I will have plenty of northern light gawking time in the months ahead, providing the laundry doesn't shrink any more pants on me. If anyone is in Truro, see if Stanfields are making a line of thermal kilt liners.

Well other than that, Jimmie is still cracking corn and my patience. The squishies are selling as well as ever, and the snowmobiling is getting better each day. I play in the community orchestra, direct a brass quartet and teach the local cadets music. And everyday, I cross my fingers, blow an eyelash into the abyss, and knock wood. This is all done in an effort to ensure I have a white Christmas. Here's to luck…

Junk Food

The amount of candy that is consumed up here is astounding, even by corner store standards. It is a common occurrence to watch kids spent $20.00 on junk food, and come back for more. I truly believe I could sprinkle sugar on the treats the cats leave in the litter box and the kids will buy it by the bag. There are pamphlets explaining to nursing women not to put pop in the baby's bottle, now that has got to be an indicator of a junk food epidemic. I know, Dr. Wong, that you made money off of me but this is a gold mine.

Luckily, the Northwest Company has stepped up to the plate and is trying to help with the problem. They have developed a Healthy Living Rewards program for the school children. By reversing the trend towards candy, the idea is to improve and prevent disease, as diabetes is a common occurrence in a lot of the hamlets. Buying a healthy snack at the Northern store will earn points for their school. The points will then be turned into cash that can be used at the northern stores for whatever the school needs or wants. The products that qualify under the program are low in fat, low in sugar, and high in fiber. They are clearly marked for the children and should definitely encourage better eating habits and a healthier lifestyle. This is a great idea as far as I'm concerned and I look forward to the results of the program. The program is only being run in Arviat and Baker Lake, but with positive results, will be expanded to everywhere a northern store exists. Currently there is a total of 174 retail stores throughout the Northern regions, and that could translate into a lot of positive energy. Good Luck to them.

On another positive note, after last week', column about missing the Northern Lights, a co-worker called to tell us that the lights were out and the lunar eclipse as well. I have only seen the lights once before, in C.F.B. Gagetown, and that was years ago. Well, that was nothing compared to what I witnessed this time. There wasn't a breathe of wind in the air, but the rolling and weaving of the night sky was like a writhing snake at times, then would darken and reappear in a vortex. It was absolutely stunning, especially with the eclipse as a backdrop. I am going to make an effort to have people call me when it happens again. Well, lets be honest, it is not like I will see it unless I drop a potato chip in front of the window.

Finally, one reader emailed an interesting point for me to ponder. He posed the question, that if Jimmie cracked corn, and nobody cared. Who would bother to write a song about it? Hmm, truly a vexing question. I would ask him myself but he is off for a few days, due to the passing of his mother-in-law and coincidently his aunt. Don't ask, I didn't…

The Two Months of Christmas

A person can't help but notice that retailers think Christmas is just around the corner. I can almost envision Water Street and Front Street with the shop windows gaily dressed for the holidays as I write. The Highland Square Mall is probably belting out Christmas songs over the speakers trying to convince the shoppers to buy, buy, and buy. Long lines of children dressed in their good clothes with over-heated, and over-stressed parents waiting to see Santa Claus. Ah, What a sight it must be. However, I can't help but wonder when the 12 days of Christmas turned into 2 months.

Two months, what the %^& is he talking about, you are probably asking yourself. Well, as you know, the Christmas shopping season begins the day after Halloween, when the kids are all hopped up on sugar. Coincidence? I think not. As everyone knows, the Gregorian calendar and other certain religious texts, having little to no commercial significance, have somehow forgotten to add " Boxing Week Blowout" and "New Year's Clearance Jamboree Sale." Add it all up and you've got a full two months of Christmas holiday shopping, leaving us all twirling and swirling into the Valentine shopping experience. But in all fairness, it is Christmas after all…

Shopping in the North does, present certain obstacles that have to be overcome. There are only a handful of stores to visit, which means in order to surprise someone with a gift that is different and unusual, it is going to have to be shipped in. Online shopping is used quite a lot. Sears, Canadian Tire, The Shopping Network are also great places to shop, as most will ship to the recipient, hence saving expensive mailing costs. My brother's gift will be shipped to my mother, my mothers to my brother, and so on and so on. It could get confusing and mind-boggling but that's what women are for, and better at. No insult intended I assure you. Women are blessed with the skill to buy gifts. They inheritably know what people want and will spend hours of exciting, pleasurable shopping in order to find it. Location is no problem; Pictou, New Glasgow, Truro, and even Halifax are well within the respectable shopping boundaries.

Men, on the other hand, can be told exactly what to buy. In some cases it can be placed right into their hands. But upon reaching the checkout, the lure of next years calendars, (golf or girls), will cause the man to put the gift down into the pile of products placed there by other lured men. Once finished the calendars the man will pick up the first thing that "feels" like the same thing he had, basically, because he wasn't paying attention when it was placed there. He was glad to have the perfect gift handed to him, and secure in the knowledge that the better half would love it. Only imagine the dismay when time to watch the surprised look on her face Christmas morning, when she opens the holiday gift box of essentially useless K-Tel products instead of the holiday gift boxed MP3 player. Hmmm, I have an idea on how to surprise Kelly. He he, this can't fail.....

The Arctic Legion

Even though Remembrance Day is over for this year, it still should be clear in the minds of those who attended services. Being a Legion member of Branch #83, Florence for nine years, a decorated officer in the CIC branch of the reserves, and having my father a veteran of WW2, RCASC; celebrating this day has been a part of my life for so long it has become as much a yearly ritual as a birthday or even Christmas. I have attended the Pictou County service for quite a number of years now, however Nov. 11 has always drawn me to

Florence, mainly due to my dear friend, and branch past president Lloyd Harris. When he sets his mind on something, lookout Nelly.

This year was the exception, for obvious reasons. So I participated in the Iqaluit Legion's service. I was asked to play the lament, and co-ordinate the Last Post. There was no street parade, however a service in both English and Inuktituk was done and done well I might add. There was a glaring difference from home and here, that was apparent to me and seemingly not many others I'm afraid. That was the lack of veterans. I realize that the rank and file of veterans is dwindling, but having only two present at the service, neither of whom spoke and one having been flown in, is a real shame. I am not blaming the Legion or anyone but I am so used to seeing veterans, putting a face to the sacrifices. I longed this year to hear a veteran draw introspective on the world's woes and try to teach policy makers the mistakes of the past in order to protect our future. Too many people today only know the hardships, sacrifices, and dangers of conflict through television. With a click of the remote they can leave the hotspots of turmoil and enter a Manhattan apartment filled with "friends", or find themselves in middle earth where a great epic is unfolding with hopes that prove good overcomes evil if the fellowship stays true. Enough said.

I just finished reading the supplement in the Advocate, the article about Nova Scotia/Nunavut command and the relationship they share in particular. There is little left to be said on that subject, however, the Iqaluit Legion is not like any Legion I've ever been to and I have been to many, many legions over the years. This Legion operates as a nightclub/dance bar. It has lineups every weekend, plays music that pumps and grinds, it is the Highlander of the North. People say "Going to the Legion" up here as commonly as they say "Going to the Tavern" in Pictou. I thought they were all crazy at first but the one time I was there, it was great. And the even greater part of it is that the profits don't go to a business, or businessperson. The profits all go to the community and worthy organizations. Hmm, I think this article needs more research, and since I am off for the weekend, tell Kelly "I'm going to the tavern, err, Legion".... for research purposes (ha ha ha).

Tough Guy

Over the years, I have been called a lot of things, funny; boy, care bear, pumpkin head, piping wiz (after I helped Trevor Kellock with his high G, he he) and a few other names not worth mentioning. But never tough guy. I often wondered why, after all I have accomplished, has this title never been conveyed upon me. Then the answer came to me one day while reading the News North. The answer was, in fact, that I am not a tough guy after all. And if I have to match this guy stunt in order to be, no thanks.

About a month ago, an Icelandic fishing captain known as the "Iceman" because of his rough and gruff character, grabbed a 300 Kg shark with his bare hands and wrestled it to the shore. The incident took place in Kuummitt in the east of Greenland. Apparently the Iceman, Sigudur Petursson, captain of the Eric The Red, was on a beach watching his crew processing a catch (whatever that means) when he saw a shark swimming towards his men, who were standing in the bloody water.

The Iceman thought his men were in danger, said a witness, so he waded out, caught the shark with his bare hands, dragged it to the beach, and killed it with his knife. Dragged and killed a 300 Kg (that's 660 lbs) shark with his bare hands! Now let me try to put this into perspective for you. This man decided that it would be wiser and more prudent to walk into the water, and do battle with a huge shark who, by the way, is in his natural environment, drag it to the beach and kill it with a knife, instead of just telling his crew to get out of the water. Now in all fairness, I wasn't there and don't fully know the entire scenario, but as far as I know that is one tough guy. Crazy, but tough nonetheless.

On a totally unrelated note; as I study the barren landscape, me thinks the annual Christmas tree hunt will be a little more difficult this year. While the Santa Claus parade went off without a hitch, the weather is really starting to dip. Days are usually -25 with wind chills to -47C.

Oh, and a footnote to a previous article about all different vehicles sharing the road, well, the other day, the Zamboni drove by the Quickie Mart on its way from one arena to the other. All I could do was shake my head and kick myself for not having my camera with me. Ha ha, a zamboni, at least the icy roads were cleaned and groomed, ready for the afternoon traffic.

A Spot of Tea

"Would you like a spot of tea?" That's a phrase often heard throughout the east coast, particularly in Nova Scotia and Newfoundland. It is as much a symbol of our identity as Maritimers as the Bluenose, Hector, or the Causeway. The first thing accomplished in most households in the morning, after the flush of course, was the kettle being boiled. My parents grew up on tea, as did my generation. An afternoon visit to my mothers still requires at least two spots, while a visit to Ira's would normally require one spot. I drink a lot of coffee now, and have for a number of years, but can't remember my last cup a tea. Which is sad. Tea seems so much more relaxing after a big meal, better for dunking toast, scones, and cookies and, oh yes, has that community/family connection for me that coffee never will. Whenever a group gathered, the tea soon followed.

Coffee is a relatively new addition to the group dynamic at community gatherings or the church hall scene, only within the last 15 years, give or take five, depending where you come from. I blame Tim Horton's for this. I dearly love Tim's. The easy access to fast brewed coffee served in an atmosphere of noncommittal meal buying, has really changed the way we operate as a society. It used to be that if you wanted a tea or coffee when you were out, you were more or less committed to a food purchase as well, which stopped a lot of people. But now, heck, I used to arrive at church with a large Tim's to play the organ on Sunday's, (three D's stupid..ha ha ha. Inside joke for Iona, and the choir at 1st Presbyterian). Up here, with the, oh the humanity, the lack of Tim Horton's, gatherings operate much like the older days of Pictou and Nova Scotia. Tea urns are the norm and people stay after events to socialize rather than escape to the nearest coffee shop, instilling a tighter group feeling and family atmosphere. Being so far away from home, I realize the most important aspect of a spot of tea was not the tea itself, but the time spent with loved ones during tea. I used to spend hours just sitting with my family, staring out the picture window, idly talking about things I know we talked about a thousand times before. The kitchen table at the Rorison's in Fox Brook or the Grants of Three Brooks were also places of great comfort and belonging. Looking back now, I can see how having a cup of tea can influence a person or community as much as a community newspaper, such as the Advocate can, by instilling a sense of family and community.

Most community newspapers will report the news highlights of their respective coverage area, but will also have colour columnists, local profiles, and an array of community groups reporting on their activities. When I read the Advocate every week, albeit usually three weeks late, I still feel like part of the community. At the end of the day, when all is said and done, the Advocate (and all community papers) is like a spot of tea...... Good for the soul....

Christmas in a Foreign Land

While I sometimes feel like I now live in a foreign country , the Christmas season brings out the best in people and highlights the similarities, not differences, we all have. The past few weeks here have been filled with Christmas concerts, visits from Santa, parades and staff parties. In short, the usual fare.

This is our first Christmas away from home and I was prepared to feel homesick not only for my family and friends but for traditions as well. I need not have feared because apparently people everywhere catch Christmas fever. The so-called kick-off began on November 29th with the Santa Claus parade. It was surprisingly good considering the dropping temperatures. (No Heatherbell's though!! Enough said) Santa of course was the highlight. It's nice having him live so close although I worry that his close proximity might mean he's keeping an even closer eye on my shenanigans than usual!

The same day played host to the annual Christmas craft fair at the high school. There is one difference from home the familiar Friday, Saturday and Sunday weekend show is crammed into 3 hours of shoving, sweating, money-spending frenzy! (Kelly loved it) The short time frame seems strange although a lady we know who's from Sackville, N.S. makes stain glass ornaments and says she sells more in one afternoon than an entire weekend at the Halifax Forum. (Sherri-Lee: you might want to plan a trip up for next year!)

Kelly brought a box of our favorite Christmas decorations with us for sentimental reasons, and because we thought holiday paraphernalia would be hard to come by and expensive. I mean, when you have to freight everything in by boat or plane, more practical things, like food for instance, take precedence right? Well, we were right about more expensive, but God love them, people here are just as impractical if not more so than home. There are lights, decorations, wreaths, and garlands, everything under the sun available. Northmart and the competition, Arctic Ventures, even sell real Christmas trees for $70.00; really not much more than you'd pay in a southern city. Kelly also bought a beautiful Christmas poinsettia at Northmart. Another holiday tradition I love. Nothing says Christmas like Kelly slowly but surely killing beautiful flowers. At last count, there are five blooms and six stalks left on the once magnificent plant. (Barbara-Ann: what DID you teach that girl?)

The city of Iqaluit hosts a 'Light it Up' contest for decorating your home. I don't think our one lighted window in the apartment is going to win us any prizes but it's a small testament to our refusal to be practical and to the winning spirit of Christmas! So, to everyone at home in Pictou County and in Cape Breton: Merry Christmas. From our home in Iqaluit to yours, we wish you all happy and safe holidays and we'll see you in the new year!

The Barter System

For many Inuit, carving is not only a tradition and a part of their heritage but also a means of living. Art galleries in the south sell carvings by well-known Inuit artisans for thousands of dollars. If you don't believe me, check out E-Bay. Most famous Inuit carvers have come out of smaller communities farther north of Iqaluit like Cape Dorset and Igloolik. However, Iqaluit itself produces a lot of beautiful and unique pieces; some by little known artists and others by people who have moved south to the "big city" of Iqaluit! (Ha ha ha ....still laughing)

At first, I wasn't sure what to think of the carvers or the people who purchase their wares. Carvers or dealers who sell for them can be found at most local restaurants and shopping stores. When I first saw these people trudging through Northmart with their goods, I fully expected someone to kick them out. I don't mean to sound callous but I know down south, business people would not allow a 'tinker' to wander their stores doing their own business. Here, this is the norm. The same people make the rounds everyday and we look forward to seeing what they have to offer. Today, they might have a nice Narwhal and some small ivory pins; tomorrow a drum dancer and some art prints.

At the restaurants and bars, the barrage is almost endless. During an average meal, one could be interrupted at least ten times. But amongst buyers, the theory goes that you get the really good deals after midnight at the Legion because sellers are more desperate for money. My fear with this practice is that what might look like a good investment after a few socials might not look quite as good come Sunday morning. (Good advice for whatever you are buying.) The other funny and kind of sad part of this local phenomenon is the carvers' bartering system. They have obviously learned over the years to be flexible with their prices but the actual art of bartering eludes them.

The Highland Square Flea Market should organize an exchange with a group of the artists to give them some lessons. A typical proposal would go like this: Robbie: "How much?" Them: "Fifty or thirty". Robbie: "Hmm, fifty dollars or thirty dollars" Now, do you see the problem with this? They obviously don't. Perhaps it stems from a native language, which doesn't seem to have numbers.

You may be thinking, 'But Robbie, you are obviously taking advantage of these poor naïve Inuit artists'. Don't worry. Nothing comes cheap up here. The artisans, while maybe bartering themselves out of twenty bucks here and there, know the value of their work. The southerners who love and appreciate their art just keep buying it. In a small city, you would think there would be market saturation at some point; that eventually, the buyers would have their fill but it is a seemingly bottomless pit. So, the carvers keep carving, the suckers, I mean southerners keep buying and everybody's happy!

Speaking of happy, I hope everyone is full of turkey. At press time, my New Year's plans were not finalized but rest assured it WILL involve merry-making and perhaps even some Auld Lang Syne-ing. Welcome 2004 Pictou County!!!

Red Light District of Iqaluit

As the holiday season starts to wrap up and the Christmas lights start to disappear, my thoughts turn to an incident of late. We were driving down to a friends place for a festive get-together and admiring the lights. The number of houses decorated with lights was far less than in Pictou, but what was out was nicely done. There were however, quite a few outdoor lights, you know the ones that look like upside-down Mason jars, and they were all glowing red.

Now I, along with fellow Pictonian, Dave Waddell, had the pleasure of visiting Amsterdam in 2000. Being a couple of Canadian hillbillies, we headed to the famous Red Light District; cameras in tow, obviously. Before I hear a bunch of "figures", we also visited the Madam Tussaud wax museum, several breathtaking cathedrals, and other notable attractions. The Red Light district was something of a bewilderment. There was a sea of people, strolling through the side alleys, along the canals, and main walkways; most of them seemingly unaware of the nature of the business being conducted. There were also quite a number of gawkers, window shoppers, and doors being opened and closed. Point of interest, no one can take a picture of the women in the windows, which are all dressed by the way, contrary to what I was led to believe.

So when I finally paid heed to the sheer number of red lights on the way that night, we started to laugh at the possibility of either a huge sale on red light bulbs, or the bawdy underside of the North finally being exposed. Pornography in any way shape or form is not sold here in the city, the reason they say, is that there are far too many other problems to deal with.

Boy, were our faces red (no joke intended) after we mingled and imparted our wonderful observations to the party guests. They all started to laugh in that good natured, look at what the greenhorn did, way that I never seem to get tired of. Apparently, because of the rough, permafrost, ground, residents have the choice of water and sewer delivery and removal in two ways; by means of above ground pipes or truck delivery. Well, if your red light is on, that tells the driver that you do not need water. Ha ha, puzzling is it not, the Dutch looked at a red light bulb and thought sex trade, the north looked at a red light bulb and thought, water delivery. Makes one wonder what the Brazilians use red light bulbs for. But in my defense, I am an apartment dweller, and knowledge about the red lights is not really an apartment thing.

Speaking of being apartment dwellers; we have been plugging our trucks block heater in faithfully for three weeks, trying to save our little workhorse from having to be put down because of the cold weather. After a quip to a neighbor about the effectiveness of our efforts, mainly because of the sluggish starts and movement, the neighbor asked if we flipped the switch on in the apartment. Yeah you know the answer to that. Actually we did notice the switch, and pulled a Monica trying to figure out what the switch operated, and just plain chalked it up to the neighbors TV set????

Sense and Sensibility

I have mentioned the freewheeling attitude of transportation in the North before, and how as long as it is registered you can use it. ATV's, cars, trucks, SUV's, Zamboni's, and even snowmobiles share the roads. The system seems to work. They all have, and enjoy, their own strengths and weaknesses.

When we arrived, we had only taxis to transport us, and thought that would be sufficient. But, the taxi industry has its own rules and Kelly has hers, you get the picture. KABOOM!!! So we bought a Honda Fourtrax to get back and forth to work, explore the land, and go fishing for the great, elusive, beast called char. But when a Suzuki Samurai (soon to be antique status) was advertised on the community bulletin board, we decided that would make sense to have it for the winter. It is quite literally a motorized soup can. None of that luxurious padded and clothed ceilings, doors, or floors for us' cause we are roughing it. Nothing but metal. The radio doesn't work, and neither does the heater, blower, windows, nor defrosters, but everything else does and well I might add. You might be wondering how we keep the trucks windows defrosted enough to drive. Well, if you don't let anyone else know, I put a ceramic heater in the truck. I ran the cord through the firewall and we run it all day and night long, plugged into the block heater. (Well, we aren't paying for the power)

But now with all the snow, cold and ice, and the constant sounds of whining engines about, everyone's minds turn to snowmobiles. The smell of two-stroke engines fill the air and with every snowfall, the bay freezes more and more. The talk at the Quickie Mart is how the rocks are being covered, making traveling farther, safer for the "sensible" operator and the snowmobile. Now when I say "sensible" don't get me wrong, I wasn't referring to me. We have now added a Bombardier 550 Legend to our stable of vehicles and it is the stallion of choice.

Fast, fun and full of heart-pounding excitement all wrapped up in two skis, a short-track and black fiber-glassed body.

Last Sunday, Yukon Jon invited me to jaunt over to Burton Bay and back. Of course I said yes without knowing the route or degree of difficulty. He didn't know the last time I drove a Skidoo, was pretty much around the tenth anniversary of Sesame Street (you can do the math if you are curious, In my mind I am still early 20's, he he) and I failed to mention it.

We headed out to Apex and started to traverse the sea-ice. Sea-ice from the shore out to about two hundred yards is very much like a stucco ceiling except bigger; very rough terrain with sharp, solid mounds of ice everywhere, and to make matters worse, in December the ice is still considered not very safe, patches of slush and water are visible yet. So as I was slaloming through the ice, I lost control and was thrown, landing on my side and lower back. Ha ha ha, I can laugh now but at the time I was really hurt. Thinking of how I faked an injury the last outing with Yukon and really couldn't turn back because of the wimp stigma that could be attached.

So I mounted the Skidoo and followed him to Burton Bay. I was so sensible to have done that. Oh, so sensible! I paid for that trip. Long story short, I am fine now, Yukon Jon eventually took one for "Team Stupid" as well that day, and the girls tell us that we can't go out and play anymore……. Probably sensible advice…

Rechargeable Batteries

One of the great things in life is the rechargeable battery. When I was growing up there was no such thing, so when the batteries died in one of our toys, it was inevitably a long time before they were replaced. My parents always had other more important things to spend their hard earned money on like putting food on the table or a roof over our heads. Phfft, what a rip for a lil boy. Ha,ha,ha, kidding. However now when the batteries die, we just plug them in, wait until they are ready and go. I think the inventors of the rechargeable battery must have looked no farther than home to be inspired. The human spirit is very much like a battery. It can and needs to be recharged every now and then.

I spent a lot of years in the CIC Reserves of the Canadian Forces and thus spent a great deal of time on the road. That was one of the perks. It got me away from what was perceived by my generation, and the youthful ones before and undoubtedly after, to be the dullest, nothing exciting ever happens here, place to live. That chorus is also sung in Pictou, New Glasgow, Antigonowhere and Iqaluit as well. I loved the opportunity to travel to different locations throughout Canada, and abroad, but always felt the same after returning. I heard my folks say time and time again; "Is it ever good to get home" or "there is no place like home." I never truly understood at the time but it was, and still is, true.

We just returned to the Great White North after spending a brief week of visiting family and friends, and we both feel rejuvenated, more positive, and closer to each other. It was a little unsettling traveling the day we came home. Ottawa airport completely changed in the four months since we had seen it last, so much so that we got lost. On the long drive to Pictou (we are used to not traveling more than five minutes anywhere now) Ira had quite the ordeal trying to maneuver the Tim's drive through at Mastodon Ridge. It is also totally changed. But once we hit Mt. Thom everything started to fall back into place. For the remainder of the week everything seemed so surreal. It surprised me how quickly the scenery and landmarks seemed like old friends again. When we drove to Cape Breton to see my family, we expected to see new things around each bend in the road, but everything was as it should be. After seven months away, life in Pictou was still the same, the jet notwithstanding.

Being home was like being placed in a battery charger. Being surrounded by loving family and friends, feeding on Stone House Pizza and Pressroom delights, (the sheer amount of fast-food I will omit fearing a backlash from the medical community, ha, ha) our spirits were fully recharged to face the world up north again.

Understanding what is important to a person is truly a gift. Not everyone knows, nor does everything mean the same thing to everyone. I am lucky enough to know what is important to me, and it is not worldly possessions. Spending time in "My Province" with family and friends, whether it is only one hour or four days. The time shared means the world to me. It was with tear filled-eyes that I left North Sydney, leaving Pictou was no different for Kelly, but the visit home and tears accomplished two wonderful things. It lifted our spirits to carry on and it strengthened our resolve to return home quickly...7 months down....

Abraham "Abe" Okpik

In Canada's North, Inuit and Eskimo are no strangers to the "civilizing" attitude of the Southerners. I mentioned before about how the Inuit used to be assigned an Eskimo number. But what I didn't tell you was that this practice was in place until 1968. Let us put that into perspective, up until a mere 35 years ago, we as a nation didn't think it important enough to know anymore about the people of this culture except for a statistic. It was Abraham Okpik that spent two years spear-heading the family name allocation project for the Inuit.

Abraham "Abe" Okpik was born in Alaska and from 1968 to 1970; he tirelessly worked to make it possible for the Inuit to drop the numbered medals that served as identification for the "Eskimos" at the time. He was an undisputed leader in the Arctic; the first Inuk to become a member of the Northwest Territories government in 1963. He died here in Iqaluit in 1997. There is a mural of him along with two others on the side of a building in Iqaluit to commemorate his achievements.

Wow, 35 years ago. That is really amazing and hard to believe. Now don't get me wrong, the government still assigns numbers to its citizens, social insurance numbers, but we are not identified solely by them and are indifferent to the fact. That is nowhere near what happened here. The Inuit were nothing more than just a number and the government didn't really seem to want to know more. Picture this scenario, the ship Hector arriving in Pictou Harbor, the Shire's leadership not bothering to try to understand their native Gaelic tongue (assuming they couldn't understand it) but instead assigning them numbers and sending them off into the woods. Up until two generations ago, your children still would have been referred to by the government as a number, not a name.

It wasn't until after this allocation period that they were identified by their surnames. However, the spellings of the surnames are still questionable. That is a history we Maritimer's share with the Inuit. When the Highland Clearances were in good swing and the Scots were descending upon New Scotland, many had little, if any, skills in the 3 R's of the time. The Scots could pronounce their names with pride but could not spell, and it was left up to the immigration officers to transcribe their names to record. Hence, the many different spellings of names that sound the same. I am reminded of the Vignette on TV with the young girl telling her name "Molly, Molly Johnson" I assume but her name could actually be Molly, Molle, Molli, Malle, Johnson, Johnston, Jonson and so on but you get the point. We are left to assume the spelling, as were most of the immigration officials. The northern experience was no different.

Abraham Okpik certainly had an arduous task ahead of him to document the entire north from "Eskimo" number to sur-name. I am happy to say that the Inuit are using surnames now. Although there is still a great deal of sorting out as to who is actually related to whom, and how the surname is actually spelled, the transition is going ahead surely as tomorrow will arrive tomorrow. Ok, they occasionally change their surname as they deem necessary (and phone numbers as far as that goes,) but considering what they as a people went through, we should forgive their flights of fancy or necessity as much as possible. After all we still have the rest of the country documented under a nine digit numbering system. Seemingly Orwell was right on the money in 1984...

Politics of Sorts

As backwards as a lot of things are north of 60, there are still elections at the municipal, territorial, and federal levels. I witnessed the municipal elections and they were the same as any I've seen in Nova Scotia. There was much to-do about issues that should have been resolved by the previous administration but only one platform that was of interest to me. One councilor proposed that if elected she would initiate a position on the council for a member of the youth. This member would bring a fresh, younger view to the issues on the table while instilling in the youth a sense of involvement in "their" community. An interesting project worthy of an honest try, me thinks.

Next month, Nunavut will be having their territorial elections and the race is interesting to say the least. In contrast to the party system in federal and provincial elections, Nunavut's consensus model of government has no parties and therefore no party leaders. Unless candidates decide to announce their intentions to be premier, or whom they would choose for the job, voters have little influence over who becomes the next government leader. That decision is left to the MLA's who elect a premier, cabinet and speaker from among themselves after the election. Next to trying to understand the American political nightmare, this has to be a close second. I have never laughed so hard at an election process in my entire life. One candidate, who has been elected by acclamation, has announced his intentions for the top seat but won't talk about his premier-platform. "That's something we discuss, the MLA's among ourselves."can you imagine John Hamm telling voters that in Nova Scotia. "No voters, you have no business knowing what my intentions are, leave that up those whom have been elected. We know best after all." Ha ha! Yeah right.

I am not saying by any stretch of the imagination that the party system is any better. In the last Liberal leadership convention in November, of the over`220,000 new members recruited, more than 30 party members were signed up from the same address, and at least one, get this, was a dead golden retriever. So do I trust a system where a deceased animal has a say in the leadership, or a system where only elected members decide the leader without the constituents knowing the platforms. Hmmmm, tough choice but thankfully I don't qualify to vote this round, due to the short, even if seemingly long, time spent living here. Not that I am complaining, I would rather stay away from this train wreck, however, it is an interesting point to note that Ed Picco, an MLA and cabinet member currently serving, and running again, is a ST.F.X. graduate.

So it seems that no matter what system of politics played, there are ways to corrupt it and bring distrust to the voters. With such a young government, this being only the first legislative assembly finishing up, the future should be bright as they have the whole history of Canada to learn mistakes from. But such an idealistic outlook is looking like folly on my part; human nature is just too strong a force to reckon with. Oh well, my memories of politics says it all, "Down wit de Causeway."

Unspoken Brotherhood

There are many unspoken brotherhoods in society, which have a slightly humorous side. These groups are not registered as non-profit organizations, they are not listed in any phone book, nor can they be found through Google or other Internet search engines. Membership is only gained by driving the proper vehicle.

Growing up in a car owning family, my first glimpse into these kinships was through the school bus. It seemed to me that all school bus drivers had the ability to instantly recognize other bus drivers whether it was another school bus, charter or Acadian lines driver, and offer a friendly wave. We all know about the transfer truck driver fraternity, a stop at a Big Stop will show anyone that they have their own lounges, shower areas, eating area, etc. But in reality, bus drivers are really only bonded by the couple of tons of metal strapped around their waists by a seatbelt.

This experience of vehicle bonding has only one exemption, one might suggest, and that is the car. Drivers of the automobile never seemed to catch on to this bonding experience. We  drive around oblivious of the fact that there are other drivers on the road, and if we bother to raise our hand to gesture to other drivers, it is usually a one-fingered wave being executed. (Long live the king, my brother, Stephen. Ha ha ha) As soon as I bought a truck, though, the gestures of acknowledgement started to come in. Drivers of other trucks would lift their fingers off the steering wheel, or slightly nod their head in respect that you have elevated yourself to the truck level. Wow, I kind of felt bad about those poor suckers still driving cars not getting noticed.

In the north, these exclusive vehicle-bonding associations apply to operators of ATV's and snowmobiles. During the high season of four-wheeling, drivers will wave to each other, check out each other's machine or clothing, and of course see who can get into the worst situation and manage to get out, and even see who can get the dirtiest. I used to watch the eyes of other drivers when someone came back into town, wearing the badge of honor of being covered head to toe in mud. You can see the minds turning "How come we don't get that dirty?" or "we have to try harder next time!" If you are stopped on the trail or road, other operators will always stop to lend a hand. But if it were a snowmobile stopped, we would just pass by, and vice versa. What is funny about this is that a lot of people in the north own both and will bond accordingly. I waved to an ATV driver while on the Ski-Doo and was seemingly snubbed. I am sure that I caught him off guard but I remember how it stood out in my mind. Nobody knows who invented the rules, or why they are even still being used, but it is a comforting feeling knowing that you are amongst friendly folks while motoring around.

Although it is now snowmobile season in Iqaluit, there are a few ATV operators still driving about. Our ATV has been put into storage and I use our Ski-Doo to run errands and explore the winter landscape. When we visited Pictou in January, Ira and Barbara-Ann were ATV operators and I couldn't really offer any friendly gestures but I am happy to welcome them with a huge wave from the North. They are new snowmobile owners and have joined yet another unspoken brotherhood.

Alcan and the RCMP

All the news revolving around the Liberals and the sponsorship program, the secrecy surrounding it, is quite entertaining. This government secrecy reminded me of the RCMP schooner St. Roch and her "voyage to firm up Canadian sovereignty in the Arctic" during WWII and to bolster Canadian pride and raise spirits. The truth of the matter wasn't actually revealed until 1992, 50 years later.

Launched in 1928, the St. Roch was built for the Arctic, carrying supplies to scattered detachments in the Arctic; sometimes she would be deliberately frozen in at some remote harbour and served as a base for officers to enforce law by way of dogsled patrols. However, during the spring of 1940, the government announced that the ship was to travel the Northwest Passage west to east, leaving Vancouver on 23 June for a scheduled arrival in Halifax, 90 days later. But she became trapped in the ice in a small bay on the Boothia Peninsula, extending the voyage into years. If the truth were told, she didn't reach Halifax until 11 October 1942. Ha ha, a 90-day tour on the St. Roch is like a 3-hour tour on the SS Minnow, or a ladies "I'll be ready in a minute."

Memos in the RCMP archives tell a different tale. It was

as the German armies marched across Europe, and Denmark fell, leaving its Greenland colonies unprotected, that Canada launched Force-X, one of it's best-kept secrets. Canada was to enter and occupy Greenland, and the St. Roch was going to provide communication and supply back up to the N.B. McLean, an Icebreaker carrying an advance party of 100 soldiers to establish an encampment until the larger contingent arrived. But why, you are probably asking yourself, Greenland. Well, we didn't do it because we were just friendly, concerned neighbors. It was entirely for business interests.

You see, the day Denmark fell under German occupation; the Aluminum Company of Canada (known now as Alcan) sent an urgent telegram to Ottawa demanding protection for the sole source of cryolite, essential in the production of aluminum. The only known mine outside of German occupation was on an isolated fiord in Greenland. Seeing how aluminum was vital to the war effort, Alcan was making a lot of money meeting the demands. If the mine were to become occupied by the Germans, the production of aluminum would grind to a halt.

One problem. Our friends south of the border, had yet to enter the war and, under the terms of the Monroe Doctrine, would be compelled to protect any country in the America's invaded by another nation. The Canadian government wasn't comfortable to test if that also meant protection against a Canadian Offensive, malicious or otherwise. So the Americans were kept in the dark as well, or so Ottawa thought. But the Americans also had aluminum production that relied on the same source of cryolite. What happened next was a major diplomatic incident. But for now, picture this; the St. Roch was only five feet longer than the ship Hector. Try to think of the Hector going to do battle with the German U-boats. Something to think about until next week, when the rest of the story unfolds.

The Greenland Stand-Off

Last week, we saw how operation Force-X was hatched in secrecy, and how the RCMP schooner, St. Roch, was making history as the first ship to travel the Northwest Passage west to east, while firming up Canadian sovereignty in the Arctic. Meanwhile, the Americans were kept in the dark about Force-X, and Canada wasn't totally sure Force-X was going to breach the Monroe Doctrine or not. The war was in swing and the war effort depended on aluminum from Alcan, which was in jeopardy from the Germans. Let's see how this all turns out, shall we.

In May of 1940, Prime Minister Mackenzie King met with President Franklin D. Roosevelt and the cat about Force-X was out of the bag. Whether the Prime Minister inadvertently spilt the beans or Roosevelt told him that they already knew isn't known. Either way, later that day, Force-X was abruptly cancelled. That, my friends, didn't bode well with the British, who relied on the aluminum. Canada went ahead with a less military plan by sending the renowned Northern Ship, the Nascopie, to appease the Brits. And the British made sure of the success by sending their own ship, a former Danish cryolite freighter Julius Thomsen across the Atlantic.

With the St. Roch and the Nascopie both heading to Greenland, the Americans thought that Force-X was being executed and dispatched one of its Coast Guard cutters, Comanche, north as well. The Comanche, Nascopie, and Julius Thomsen all met in the fiord leading to the cryolite mine. High-level diplomats from the nations involved all met for intense discussions, while the ships laid in wait.

Now in the movies, the RCMP would have arrived at the last minute and resolved the dispute in the professional and respectful manner that is their international trademark. But the

RCMP, and the St. Roch were trapped in ice 2000 kilometers away. What happened next is still unclear, but three weeks later, the Nascopie was allowed to load cryolite and leave. Rumor has it that it wasn't diplomatic talks that got the ship loaded, but a generous amount of booze from the Canadian crew that sealed the deal for the miners to load the cryolite. Ha ha ha, at least some things never change.

The relationship between the RCMP and Alcan was rekindled again in 2000, when the Aluminum Company of Canada said thanks to the St. Roch by making a sizeable donation to the preservation of the schooner, currently on display at the Vancouver Maritime Museum. Well done.

The moral of the story is that very little of what the government tells us is in fact, the truth, the whole truth, and nothing but the truth. We, as citizens, should always strive for transparency in government, whether it be the sponsorship scandal or not. We live in the greatest province, in the greatest nation on earth, and we shouldn't be represented by anything less.

Oh Where, Oh Where Have my Numbers Gone

Growing up and living in Nova Scotia, we have become accustomed to teaching and learning our numbers. By the time most children attend primary, they have a good grasp on numbers from one through ten. It is essential for us to have a numerical system for financial, scientific, and just plain, ole, social reasons. Everyone knows how many in our families, how many children our friends have, etc, etc. The Inuit and the Inuktitut language, both verbal and written forms, use English numerals.

The numerous articles found in newspapers, documents, what have you, that are written in Inuktitut, would look something like this "φηφκαηη ηφηονιηκ νκφη 1998 ηφκφ ιοιοη" Mind you I don't have Inuktitut script on my computer but you get the idea. The verbal language is no different. A typical conversation would sound like, no insult intended, " Anuk nuk siak oopallee 1998 goowalla nuk anuk." Ha ha ha, the English numbers really stand out. It baffles my mind as to why this has happened.

How could a culture, and community survive, without having a system of numbers? One would think that at some point during, lets say a caribou hunt, one Inuk would ask how many days they are going to be on the land, how many children his hunting partner has, how many caribou there were in a herd in yonder tundra. And when they returned, what would they say to each other. Wife says, "Hi dear, how far did you go to get this undisputed amount of meat." "Well, sweet pea, me and the boys went as far as bigger than a puddle lake and found them." Meanwhile holding his arms open wide showing her a visual for the amount, kind of like Ira and Roy explaining to us the size of the one that got away.

I have asked around and never found an acceptable

answer as of yet. Most people have noticed the missing numbers but never thought about it beyond that. One solution was that when the missionaries put the language into script, they just used English. But that doesn't explain the oral form. I have asked Ole Cracked Corn, but after a minute of his Caribou-caught-in-the-headlights-of-a-skidoo look, I move on to a different topic. Usually his new money making venture, seeing how his recycling washers and dryers project never really got off the ground. Ha ha ha good ole Jimmie. Always leave them laughing.

I figure eventually that this could go all the way to the Legislative Assembly of Nunavut, as the elected wise men explain to the unsuspecting constituents that the reason we have such a huge deficit after only one session is that they have grown up on not having a Inuktituk system of numbers. Now that they had to deal in the English system of numerals, a Foreign concept, they were unaware how it operated. Too bad Paul Martin couldn't use the same excuse in his Adscam problem.

Next week, I will explain why it is better to have piles in the North, as compared to in Pictou.

The Piles

1-2-3-4-5-6-7. During a period where the media is getting hit with a series of time delays; Coach's Corner, the Oscars, etc., my column is no different. The editor has imposed a 7 second delay on me. That is why the column seemed to start slightly after I started to type it. Ha ha, I kill me. But seriously, moving on.

When I was growing up my mother used to constantly warn me, (while pointing her right index finger at me) "Robbie!! Stop eating your crayons and don't be sitting on those cold, damp cement steps. They will give you the piles."

I'm not even sure the crayons were non-toxic back then (Hmmm, that might explain the night terrors. Mental note, research crayons) and I never understood what the piles were either but as I got older the old light bulb got brighter. There were more references to the piles and how to avoid getting them. I was told on good authority that if your face starts to contort and turns beet red, and you start to sweat profusely during the fifth movement in the 'john', oh yeah, you could get the piles. So really, in Nova Scotia having the piles is not a great thing, however in the Arctic, that is a different story. Let me explain.

As one gazes over the city and hamlets of the north, you will undoubtly see that all the houses and buildings are on stilts.  It took me awhile to figure out why that was. In the process I found out that they are not stilts, in fact they are called piles and everyone in the North has them. You see, because the land is comprised mainly of sand, (hence the term Arctic desert), and it is in a state of permafrost, builders can't put in a basement or build on the ground. Why you ask, well because the amount of heat loss through the basement or footing would cause the ground to thaw. The sand would then compress and the building would shift and sink into the ground causing major structural damage. So buildings are erected on piles to allow the wind to whisk the heat loss away. Pretty smart eh. The only exceptions to the practice are the buildings constructed directly on bedrock, and there are some.

The holes for the piles are dug out, the piles are then placed into the holes surrounded by sand and then soaked with water. After three days the sand has refrozen and the piles are permafrostly held in place. The only drawback to the process is that the buildings tend to sway in the winds. We have pretty much given up on sun catchers in the windows, way too noisy as they constantly knock on the glass. Some people actually use their toilets as an indicator of whether work or events are cancelled or not. They glance in the bowl during their morning ablutions and if the water is pulsing, in and out of the bowl (and it does) they know that cancellations are coming for the day. Ha ha ha. Another great use for the porcelain dish.

Rumor has it that Pictou's own Dave Gunning will be traveling to the Great, White, Metropolis of Iqaluit this spring. Troy and Kendra MacGillivray will accompany him. Everyone can hardly wait for their arrival. Dave will definitely show Iqaluit what Pictou talent is all about and in the process create an interest in tourism for Pictou. Well it looked as if I got through another column without being censored, ha ha, I think…. 4-5-6-7

Eskimo Pies

After months of investigative reporting, and a much larger waistline, I am happy to announce that those delicious Eskimo Pies are made of ice cream and not Eskimos. This marketing image of the Eskimo certainly doesn't infer that they are made of actual Eskimos but if blueberry pies are made of blueberries, and rabbit pies are made with rabbit, well you can follow the logic. The popular image of the northern face, surrounded by fur has been around for over a century in advertising and used for a multitude of product and service marketing.

The Nunatta Sunakkutaangit Museum recently held an exhibit of Madeleine and Jae Redfern's collection of advertisings. They were inspired by a similar exhibit in Hull, Quebec, at the Museum of Civilization based on "Indians". I could never have imagined the diversity of products that were sold over the years using the Northern image. Internet to mortgages in Great Britain to peaches were all there. Kimberley-Clark has even used the Eskimo as a marketing tool to sell paper. The use of the northern people in advertising was not always positive over the years either. They were quite a few derogatory comments used to market products that, in hindsight should embarrass the marketers. The exhibit is gone now but the Redfern's have plans to collect more ads and eventually publish a coffee table book, with hopes of collaborating on a documentary film. This show has sparked an interest in quite a few people, myself included.

Living in Nova Scotia, with its rich Scottish history, made me think back to how our Celtic heritage has been employed over time. From The Macdonald Lass, used to sell tobacco in the past, to the recent Where's Wallace Piper doing the Marilyn Monroe in order to sell Pepsi's Sierra Mist. (Ha ha ha I personally think the commercial is extremely funny and I laugh my lower back off every time, especially at his high pitched squealing, but I have to agree with the young lad,

"That's just wrong" ha ha ha I hope the Hector Festival or New Scotland Days this season doesn't inspire any re-enactments.) It does show the range of possibilities explored by advertisers using the Scottish culture. And in this regard, I found yet another aspect of how the bond between Nunavut and Nova Scotia grows closer. They both have cultures that are easily recognized around the world. One quick look at the kilted highlander or the fur-trimmed parka wearing Eskimo, and it conjures up a multitude of emotions, prejudices and expectations in the viewer.

I hope that eventually in Nova Scotia, whether it is an individual, or a class project, the collection of the numerous advertisings will be started exploring the impact it has upon us. I look forward, hopefully, to an exhibit when I return. In the meantime, I must try to lose this waistline. I think I actually passed out the other day, bending over to tie my shoes. Onward into the night.

Nunavut Snow Challenge

The annual Nunavut Snow Challenge is not exactly what you think; we are not challenging anyone to record the most snow. Nunavut has a dry climate overall, so the amount of snowfall is minimal compared to Pictou. What we do get stays, and stays. At the present, I would suspect Pictou has received about three to four times the snow compared to the North, and you can keep it. This Snow Challenge is an annual snowmobile race, and quite a grueling one at that.

The Nunavut Snow Challenge starts out in Iqaluit, travels 160 km along a centuries-old trading route to Kimmirut. At an average speed of over 100 km/hr, racers leave the starting line two by two, at 15 second intervals. They cross the sea ice on Frobisher Bay before they brave the mountain passes and riverbeds of the Meta Incognita Peninsula. Not for novice riders, I guarantee you. There are hidden rocks, ice ruts, treacherous pack ice, and severe cold weather. Frostbite is always present with weather hovering anywhere from -20 to -40C, before the wind chill factor. It was -65C the last couple days with the wind-chill, and let me tell you folks, that is $%$ing cold. The race also pushes the snowmobiles, while state-of-the art, to the limits of their speed and endurance.

I took my 550 Legend across the bay for a spin. It is 27 km from shore to shore, and it took me about 30 minutes, then we went along the trail to Kimmirut to the first cabin, another 20 minutes. It was a really beautiful drive, but still I was traveling at what is considered by most drivers a reasonable speed. This race was completed last year in 3 hours and 2 minutes. There are a lot of snowmobiles traveling along the route during the year and it usually takes around 4 hours, one way. These racers are doing the return trip in just over three.

Last year there were 38 brave racers and this year is shaping up to be better. Race day is set for 27 March, and is being filmed by Nunavut Productions, with the help of TSN. TSN and OLN will be broadcasting the event on the 17-18 Apr. So if anyone is interested in watching the racers, with a spectacular backdrop of the Arctic geography of Baffin Island. Tune in on those days, it promises to be a great show.

With the Snow Challenge also arrives the Northern Pikes for the opening concert and Ed the Sock for the closing ceremonies. The event has been a highlight of the North for a number of years now, as it showcases Iqaluit, the Inuit culture and community, and the beautiful nature of the Nunavut Territory.

I was going to enter the race, cut a few Pictou Advocate labels out of the newspaper and stick them to my machine, wave to the crowd and cameras as I take off from the starting line. However, the $200 entry fee was a wee bit too much to pay for the national exposure of my pathetic display. It would have been a lot of camera time, as you would see, eventually, everyone pass me both on the way to Kimmirut and back. Ha ha ha ha. Next year maybe. This year I will be in the crowd with our Pictou sign that Gordon MacAloney wood scrolled for us before we left.

New Job

Every good thing in life, eventually comes to an end. As of the 22 March, I will not be working side by side with Ole Jimmie Cracked Corn at the QuickStop. I have fantasized about this for a long, long time. I have run the moment over in my head a thousand times. What I would say to him, how would he react to the news? Could I actually get through the whole thing without a huge smile on my face, jumping up or down, or skipping through the aisles in jubilation?

When the day arrived, I did do it without the anticipated antics of a child. I guess I have matured, in public anyway. We laughed, we cried, we held hands. You know the usual stuff people do in these situations. It was like a sitcom retrospective. I had "The Time of My Life" playing in the background, while the memories of he and I battling wits flashed through my mind. Good times my friends, good times.

Moving on... back in 1864, a group of enterprising Halifax merchants agreed to enter into a co-partnership to "discount promissory notes and acceptances, make advances on approved securities, purchase and sell bills of exchange, receive money on deposit, and transact all other business matters connected with a banking establishment." In 1869, the bank received its federal charter and was incorporated under the name of the Merchants' Bank of Halifax. However, in 1901, it became apparent that in order to reflect it's growing continental aspirations, and to avoid confusion with the Merchants' Bank of Canada, they needed to change their name to the more distinctive The Royal Bank of Canada. The banks legal name was shortened in 1990 to Royal Bank of Canada. Finally, in 2004, they put the crowning jewel in their corporation; they asked me to join their organization.

Besides the obvious increase in pay and benefits offered,

the best thing about the job change is that it will provide me with training in a job that can be transferred back to Nova Scotia. I am starting as a Customer Service Representative (teller) but the branch has been designated a training branch due to its location, which not all branches are. Opportunities are only limited to my ambition and motivation, intelligence notwithstanding.

Ironically, up to now, I couldn't tell you much about the banking biz as Kelly controlled the purse strings. I would have to work every payday, while Kelly would be off. By the time 10:00 am rolled around, she would have been on-line already and drained it all into bills or whatever. If someone asked me if I received all my pay, or how much I was paid, I would respond, "you are talking to the wrong person. See this ring, this is not the Legendary Ring of Power, the one ring that rules them all". Oh no. Precious is sitting next door, with the glow of the computer screen gleaming through the many facets and carats as it bounces up and down on the keyboard. You would have thought someone would have warned me. Ira, he never even hinted at it. I guess all the married guys thought, why should they suffer alone? Well let me tell you this, the next time someone is getting married, I will be the first person there-with my mouth shut....

Tartan Day

April 6th is officially recognized as Tartan day in Nova Scotia and abroad, which commemorates all the best in Scottish  history and culture. It is a day to proudly display your Celtic heritage by donning a kilt or wearing a piece of tartan during your daily activities. But did you also realize that the date was chosen because it marks the anniversary of the Declaration of Arbroath, the Scottish Declaration of Independence signed in 1320 at Arbroath Abbey on the east coast of Scotland. I thought not, well fasten your seatbelts, here we go.

The Declaration is without doubt the most famous document in Scottish history. It is considered by many to be the founding document of the Scottish nation, and in an interesting side note, the American Declaration of Independence is actually partially based upon it. This Declaration sent to Pope John XXII in April or May of 1320, widely believed to have been drafted by Abbot Bernard in the scriptorium of Arboreta Abbey, was on behalf of the nobles and barons of Scotland. The document received the seals of several barons and it then was taken to the papal court at Avignon in France by Sir Adam Gordon in attempt to abate papal hostility. But was it a cunning diplomatic letter or a document in constitutional thought, or both?

There has been a lot of debate over this question. For some it is simply a diplomatic document, while others see it as a radical shift in western constitutional thought. Those for the diplomatic letter side see the Declaration as a cunning ploy by the barons to explain and justify why they were still fighting their neighbors when all Christian princes were supposed to be united in their crusade against the Muslims. Government trying to mask greed by paperwork. Sound familiar? On the other hand, others saw the document as not only one of the most eloquent expressions of nationhood, but also the first expression of the idea of contractual monarchy. You see, the Declaration threatened to drive Robert the Bruce out if he ever sold out Scotland to the English. It was a grand bluff of course, as there was no replacement for him at the time, but the point was that the nobles and clergy based their arguments to the Pope not on the traditional idea of the Divine rights of Kings. Robert the Bruce was King first and foremost because the nation chose him, not God, and the nation would just as easily choose another if they were betrayed by their King.

Regardless of the motivations for its creation, the Declaration of Arbroath, under the extraordinary circumstances of the Wars of Independence, was a prototype of contractual kingship in Europe. So yet another reason for us to proudly wear our family, Provincial, or Ship Hector tartan on Tartan Day, and yes I realize it was yesterday but humor me anyway. Even though Nunavut is the only province or territory that doesn't have its own official tartan, the process has begun. Maybe next year there will be an unveiling to announce. In the meantime I will leave you with an extract from the Declaration that still rings true for Canadian Peacekeepers today; "It is in truth, not for glory, nor riches, nor honours that we are fighting, but for freedom - for that alone, which no honest man gives up but with life itself."

The Playoffs

Well another year has passed and we are into the play-offs once again. Pictou County has a strong and vibrant hockey community whether it is on the ice or in front of the tube. At this time of year it seems everybody has something to say about hockey. Team loyalty seems to be spread quite evenly, albeit the original six still carry the majority of fans, however the remainder have garnered a lot of support as well. In Iqaluit there seem to be only three teams that appear worthy of support. The Nashville predators have a strong following, not because of the team but because of Jordin Tootoo. He has overcome such tremendous challenges on his journey to the NHL. He is seen as a hero to the youth of the North, and a symbol of what can be achieved with hard work and determination. All that said, in Iqaluit, the hopes of the cup remain on Ottawa, Toronto, or Montreal.

I don't fully understand the reasons for seemingly only three team loyalties. I can only assume it has to do with the close proximity of the teams in regard to their location. The only two flights out of Iqaluit going south are to Ottawa and Montreal. Toronto is close enough to qualify as one could easily visit. It stands to reason that when people get the chance to go south, it is always nice to catch a game starring your favorite team, hence my theory. Around town there are lots of team jerseys, license plates, hats and jackets, and there are also an enormous number of team flags hanging from car windows. That you don't see in Pictou. There is other team paraphernalia for sale, as I have witnessed, but if anybody does buy it, they must only display their pride in the comfort of their homes, as I have yet to find any Bruins, Devils, Red Wing or other fans in public anywhere. I always joked by saying that two things seldom used in Iqaluit are fifth gear and common sense. So I suppose the invisibility of those fans is the exception that proves the rule. Anyway, I digress, I need not say where my team loyalty stands, as I think 24 Lord Stanley victories says enough already, and I fit in with Northern hockey allegiances well. I do though have to mention a little more on the Leafs though.

Now I have a lot of Toronto fans in Pictou County for friends (Dave Waddell, Trevor Rorison and Trevor Kellock to mention but a few), and often pondered why that was. Could it be that I have a need to try and help them see the light? Maybe, but I think is has more to do with the fact that I have a soft spot for them. Every year they approach the playoffs with such enthusiastic, naïve optimism. It kind of reminds me of Charlie Brown's Linus waiting for the Great Pumpkin to appear. It's sort of cute; really it is, in a sad way. No matter how disappointing the results, I know that next season they will be back to go through it all over again. I know I mentioned much earlier in the year that I was living in hells half-acre and it was frozen, drawing conclusions to the Leafs winning the cup this year, well I guess we will see, but I know for a fact that the Great Pumpkin didn't appear this year so……

Toonik Tyme

I was starting to think that there were only two seasons in the north, one looong, looong winter and one short summer. But as I become aware of the little idiosyncrasies of the Arctic, I realize, contrary to my previous belief, that there is actually a spring. Mind you it is not the beautiful spring we are used to experiencing in Pictou, with crocuses and tulips blooming, the return of the red breast robins and eventually the distinct color and aroma of lilacs. No, here in the North the way to tell when spring arrives is when it actually gets warm enough to snow again. I know, sad to say but true. The last couple of days it was snowing so seemingly, spring has sprung in Iqaluit. With the arrival of this new season, comes the festival of spring, better known as Toonik Tyme.

As I see it, ToonikTyme is Iqaluits' equivalent of Lobster Carnival, except for the parade, beer tent, midway, warm weather, but I digress.

Like the Carnival it is the most anticipated, largest and longest festival we have. In traditional folklore, the "tuniq" would herald spring's arrival, he is a sort of like the Arctic Easter Bunny. For years, he would appear around town dressed in Caribou skins, during Toonik Tyme and if spotted, you could call the Toonik Tyme Hotline for a chance at prizes. I never heard if the tuniq will be around this year or not but I suspect he will make an appearance.

During Lobster Carnival, (which I will be attending this year, Yayy) Pictou has it usual array of events, and so does

Iqaluit but with a more northern flair. We will be celebrating the arrival of spring with a snowmobile poker rally, oval and drag racing, an ice sculp-

ture and igloo building contest, as well as seal hunting and skin-
ning competitions. And what spring festival would be complete
without a sea-ice golf tournament. Is it just me or does there
seem to be a lot of "Spring" events dealing with snow and ice.
And of course, there are multiple bingo games, craft sales and
the 2nd annual game of Fear Factor.

I will be taking in quite a few of these events, as I feel it
necessary to prepare for the upcoming carnival. The Fear Factor
has definitely piqued my interest level. In a culture where eating raw caribou, sometimes from old caches from under rocks
on the land, the stakes must really be high in order to create a
level of challenge and fear. I can hear it now "Alright, ladies
and gentlemen, Jimmie here has to eat this plate of caribou eye-
balls in order to stay in the game." Jimmie's response, "You
guys are awful skimpy with the portions, I thought I was supposed to be eating something weird tonight." I guess I will have
to wait and see. In the meantime, I will just have to continue on
with the northern experience and count the days until the sound
of pipes fill the air, and beds race down the street.

Astro Hill Complex

Everyone, at some point, has no doubt wished that they didn't have to face the elements of winter on a daily basis. The early mornings clearing the walk and driveway of snow, warming the car up, and battling snow-covered, icy roads to get to work and, of course, back home again later. If you live in Iqaluit, however, you have a choice. You can do the former, or you can just hop on your snow machine and forego the snow removal and dangerous roads. I can envision some American film crew documenting the process. The voice hushed on tape so as not to make his presence aware to us, "Now watch as these hardy Canadians bundle up and take to their snowmobiles as they make their way to their various occupations in the Territorial capital." Or if the cold weather is just not your cup of tea, you could make camp at the Astro Hill Complex.

There is no place in Pictou that could even compare to the Astro Hill Complex. This complex was built in the 70's and houses quite an impressive list of amenities. There is a hotel, restaurant, video store, swimming pool, pharmacy, convenience store, bar and grill, apartments, conference center, ATM, government offices, CBC radio, coffee stand, clothing store and a movie theatre with two screens. There are stories told about how some people never step outside the complex during winter, as everything they could want or need is there. They live in an apartment in the eight-story building, work within the complex, shop, eat and relax all without stepping out into the cold. I am not sure if there is any truth to the stories, but quite conceivably you could do just that.

The complex is quite visible from any angle around the city and used by just about everyone. The restaurant is quite pricey but what else is new in Iqaluit. The bar and grill used be on the opposite side of the complex and called the Zoo, but after a major renovation, the new facility, called the Storeroom, was opened last summer and hosts a lot of games as well as serving food. The biggest draw to the complex has to be the Astro Hill Theatre. The theatre itself definitely shows its age, the speakers are antiquated, as is the décor. Every time I go there I am some-how reminded of the TV show M*A*S*H* and the way they used to watch movies in the mess tent. Ha ha, It is not that bad of course, but coming from the multiplex theatre in New Glasgow to here is something of a huge step backward for mankind

.

The theatre has opened a second screen this year, much to its credit. Now we have a choice of two movies to watch. The second screen is much smaller than the original because it is housed in a remodeled conference room, The movie-line is the funniest aspect to it. If anyone has time on their hands and a long distance telephone plan, you have to call the movie-line and listen to the owner as he explains what movies are playing, along with his colorful comments about each. He has a British accent and an obviously unscripted dialogue which at times has language that can be a little harsh for younger callers, but all in all it is definitely worth the call. I usually call two or three times a week, as the message changes daily. I am never disappointed or left without a smile on my face. The number is 411 under Astro Hill Theatre.

To My Friend

Everybody receives bad news and there are no exceptions. We all know this about life. The trouble is we never get any better at preparing for it. Thursday was no exception; a really close friend of mine was tragically taken away from me and the world via a motorcycle accident. Nova Scotia will be missing something special with this tragedy and the fabric of society will be dulled ever so slightly forever.

I first met Zach Warden in Halifax at a pipe and drum workshop. He stood out in the crowd by being not only a talented piper but a great leader as well. If I had to describe him in one word, it would be 'Attitude'. He had such a self-confident attitude; he was never one to back down from a challenge and always achieved his goals. Zach, as well, possessed a positively infectious atti-

tude that could not be suppressed. He made everyone feel like they truly belonged. Zach could get a group of people to shovel manure and enjoy it. It was always a pleasure to work with him and I considered him in my inner circle of friends. He made quite a number of trips to New Glasgow to lend his skills and abilities to 219 RCACC Pipe band and never once looked for remuneration. He was always there to listen and offer advice either personally or musically. Unfortunately, that being said, I am isolated in the North and will not be present for the funeral.

Growing up in North Sydney, I never thought about being isolated and cut off from the world, even though all it would take is the Canso causeway being shut down. When I moved to Pictou, and did contract work at Michelin, I worried quite often about the causeway being closed and not being able to arrive at work on time. But living in Iqaluit has made any previous worries seem childish and minor. Life in the north is truly a test of ones ability to endure isolation. The only way in and out is by airplane, and that fact is never far from anyone's mind. The Iqaluit Airport or the 'Yellow Submarine' as it is also known, is one of the busiest per capita in North America. There is a steady stream of planes arriving and departing daily. The fact that anything medically challenging must be flown to Ottawa is always a concern. For those living in Nova Scotia, the unfortunate news of a funeral can be difficult but one can travel by bus, car, plane etc, to bring themselves comfort, support and of course closure. Closure is what I will be missing here. I am in the unfortunate position of not being able to come home for the funeral. A fact that will bother me for a long time, I am sure.

Well if there is a moral to this story, here is it. Never wait another moment to tell the people you love how you feel. Ensure that they know it after each time you meet, either in person or otherwise. Zach had a way of wearing his heart on his sleeve, and never had to tell people how he felt because you always knew. I am the opposite, I have a difficult time expressing my heart but it is never too late to change I suppose. Here goes, Pictou, I love your charm, people, and hospitality. I am proud to be a resident and look forward to many years of being held within your community. And Zach, I loved you too; I and all of Nova Scotia will miss you dearly. Heaven is sounding a lot sweeter tonight as another great piper falls into the band.

Potholes and Mud-puddles

Now that spring has arrived, the roads in Iqaluit are simply a mess. I remember the good old days driving in Nova Scotia and complaining about the potholes, Never again. You guys are driving on luxurious roads compared with us. At least during the winter, the roads up here were smooth because the holes were all filled with hard packed snow. But now it is next to impossible to drive anywhere much faster than 15 km/hr. The city has graders that resurface the roads at least twice a week, so at least we don't bite our tongues off or shatter our teeth driving for eight days a month. However, that is a small price to pay for warmer weather.

The days are definitely longer as we travel through the month of May. It is daylight at 4 am and gets dusk at 9:30 pm. Very soon I won't see the dark at all for a while, and that is alright as well because, as I just mentioned, the days are getting warmer. I never thought that I would ever call -15 a nice, mild day, but after a winter of -60 temperatures, the days really do seem nice and mild. With it come the ATV's out of storage. We took ours out Sunday for a drive around. It was really nice to drive it again, even if it is a dirty and sloppy adventure. There are a lot of puddles and slush around; for the next couple of weeks the capital of Nunavut will be a huge mud hole. When I come in from a ride, I`ll be covered in mud, sort of like when I was young. I can almost hear my mother scolding me, "Joseph, Joseph, Joseph, look at the state of those clothes. Scandalous, I hope the neighbors didn't see you looking like that." Ah Mother's Day memories from away.

It will soon be time to put the Skidoo away for the summer, but not yet. The bay is still frozen and there is lots of snow on the land for playing. I suspect there will be about three more weeks to go. I remember arriving last year in May, seeing all the snow and wondering, what did I get myself into this time. As time went on, I realized that the snow does leave, albeit only for a short time and there is a summer season in the North. As long as we keep busy, time goes by quickly which makes next month and our long awaited vacation back home just around the corner. It will be so nice to see everyone, we are especially excited to see little Evan Talbot again, and his new niece Madison. Congratulations Brooke and Mike, we wish you all the best.

Last but not least, the Great Pumpkin didn't arrive again this year and neither did the cup for my friends. All I can say is, Ha ha ha. Big surprise!

Down Home Concert

Wow, what a night. Saturday evening at the Cadet hall starring Troy, Kendra, Sabra MacGillivray, and none other than the pride of Pictou, Dave Gunning. They put on a wicked concert filled with great music and a mix of homegrown humor. I overheard a gentleman saying that Dave should be on Yuk-Yuks. They were a tremendous hit and everyone there definitely had a true Maritime experience. There were square dancers and step dancers on the floor for most of the performance. I might be mistaken, but I think an enthusiastic lady threw her long underwear on the stage at Dave. Ha ha ha

It will be almost a year since I arrived in the North and thought it would be interesting to see what impressions the North has brought to another resident of Pictou. Usually after a while a person accepts their surroundings as state of normalness. So I asked Dave a couple of questions to see if my perspective has changed all that much since last year. Dave told me that he arrived in Iqaluit without any preconceived notions and with an open mind. The landscape being so barren was something that stood out in his mind. Looking back at my arrival, we have that in common. However being here less than a week, Dave said he was impressed by the strength and character of the Inuit. The way their culture is sustaining itself in the midst of constant change, and the influences of other cultures. He remarked at how a young Inuk danced his traditional dance to Dave's Maritime music. A fusion of cultures both respecting the other. Quite remarkable.

I related the vision of the Real Northern News to Dave; to strengthen the pride in the community of Pictou County, to serve as a reminder of how good we actually have it in the county and to remind me, on weekly basis, what is waiting for me to come home to. That is something he had no problem relating to, traveling a lot has taken him to a great many places but he's always found strength in his heritage and music to find his way home again.

It seems after a year in the Arctic, my perspective is still the same, and my focus is still on returning home.

Sitting back and watching the sea of dancers celebrating their different cultures together reminded me of a box of crayons. There are a lot of different colors, a wide variety of names, some sharp, some not so sharp; all together in the box for a purpose. If one is missing, a potential masterpiece can never be completed. Dave reminded me of something similar, he related how Peter Zowski once said that every Canadian should visit the North at least once, to make the experience of being Canadian complete.

Hiking Day

Victoria day weekend has come and gone, basically celebrated the same up here as home, with a few exceptions: two days of snowfall, snowmobiles on the sea ice, ATV's on the land and only one tent set up for hiking day. Victoria day weekend in Nova Scotia has been known as hiking day weekend for as long as I can remember. A weekend where everyone gets out into the great outdoors and enjoys what Mother Nature does best.

As a young lad growing up, (the middle child between Judy and Stephen), we used to watch Mom pack a lunch bag of peanut butter sandwiches, a bottle of pop usually from the ole Pop Shoppe (I wonder sometimes if I am the only one who remembers that) and a treat of some sort. We would put it all in Judy's bike basket and head out the Johnson's Road for an adventure. This would consist of biking in a sea of other bikers, hikers and strollers on the old dirt road. We would get about one kilometer out and Judy would call it quits, meaning of course that the adventure would quit as well, because she had the lunch.

In Pictou, Kelly tells me that they used to go fishing every Victoria Day weekend, at some undisclosed, clandestine fishing hole that Ira kept secret. All she can remember is that it was near a large gravel pit out Mabou way. I know what an avid sportsman he is and believe he might have doped them up on turkey and then blind folded them so they could not disclose the location during girl talk later with friends. Ha ha ha, I am kidding of course about the turkey, not quite sure about the blind-folds yet. Hmmmm.

Driving around, yes driving and not hiking, biking or anything else requiring energy, the city and greater Iqaluit area (i.e. the dump and airport) we met a lot of hikers, and bikers all enjoying the day. I believe that it has to do with the strong

Maritime flavour here. John Graham, the Airport Manager, who just last week had a great meal at Relics on route to his Legion meeting in Port Hawkesbury, tells me that it is a huge camping weekend in Iqaluit. So everything said and done, whether you live in Cape Breton, Pictou or the Arctic, everyone has the same idea for the long weekend in May, enjoy the great outdoors.

Oh, by the way, I had two choices to make about my ever, expanding waistline. I could either exercise and go on a diet, or just accept the fact that my kids will call me Fat Ba#$%d, like in Austin Powers, when I get older. I chose the latter because it took less energy and I really have no one to impress anymore. Also I can always ground the kids for using foul language. I call it my "Eat, drink and be merry, with a possibility of scientists finding a miracle weight loss pill in the future diet." Well, they put a man on the moon didn't they????He he he

For Sale

I remember many trips to Sobeys, walking by the Community Bulletin Board without even glancing or giving it much of a passing thought. As a matter of fact, I never really paid much attention to any bulletin board over the years, but since living here I've realized they are powerful selling tools in Iqaluit. Everything can be found on the many boards within the capital. There is at least one in virtually every commercial building.

The postings are constantly changing and range from vehicles of all types, housing rentals, to job opportunities; all the way to Iqunaq-fermented walrus meat. (Mmmmm Yummy) There are a lot of "Iqaluit bargains" to be found on the walls. Objects sell for twice as much as they would in Pictou. As the city is fairly transient, 'Moving' or 'Everything Must Go' sales are quite common and attended by a lot of people. Most items on the boards are sold within the week, and some, like walrus tusks for $100, won't last a day. I find myself looking at the board at work at least twice a day always finding something different and interesting. The Iqunaq is selling for $50 and is still for sale if anyone is interested. I should buy some for Kelly; our wedding anniversary is the end of the month. If the first is paper, 25th, silver and gold for 50, I wonder what anniversary calls for fermented walrus meat. I can see her face now. At least the couch is comfortable.

We have bought quite a number of things; truck, bookcase, printer, filing cabinet; and I found my new job at the Royal Bank all on the bulletin boards. Not bad for a 4 x 6 piece of cork.

Speaking of the Royal Bank, about two weeks ago, the RBC automated teller system went down across the country due to communication lines trouble. Whew, all I remember from that day was that is was busier than normal, and I was punching buttons and pushing different keys on the computer, then the system went wacky. Now I realize that the Royal Bank would never let someone as technologically inept as me come even remotely close to such a situation but the thought definitely has Robbie written all over it. Picture it; the whole automated banking system being shut down when I'm trying to change foreign currency to Canadian. "Lets see here, madam, 50 Euro dollars will equate to approximately $100 Canadian, enough for two Iqunaq's. Now all I do is press this red button and the transaction will be complete." TADA!!!!!

A bulletin board is also located outside the Pictou Post Office

Mush, Mush!

On Tuesday evening we experienced an opportunity of a lifetime, dog-sledding in the North. John Laird, a piper and a gentleman, owns a team and offered us a ride up the bay. The day was bright, sunny and warm by Iqaluit standards. We met John at the end of what they call the causeway, which we would call service road in Pictou. Regardless it is the safest way onto the sea-ice this time of year.

We were first introduced to Nunatuk and Ester. They  came to the site with John because Ester is in the process of being bred and Nunatuk got quite a scuffing last week from the other boys on the team and he had to be isolated for a period to mend and give the others a cooling off. Because Inuit dogs are bred to maintain their bloodlines, they are still very aggressive when the mood strikes them. The aggressive line is con-sidered a bonus because, as our host illustrated, the dog's love to run and pull. Characteristics which make the team do it to the point of collapse. A definite, bonus years ago in a time when dog teams were the main source of transportation and the weath-er extremely cold.

As we approached the sea-ice there were eight other teams hitched who all started to howl and bark. John was busy trying to keep

101

Esker and Nunatuk from the other teams. We arrived at our team and were shown the way and the reason they were all separated and anchored to a central hitch. There was Larry, Curly and Moe, the bruisers of the group. Then there was Pingo, Rosie, Pumanee and Piguaq. We were taught how to attach harnesses to each dog and the best order to attach them to the kamotiq. Each dog is like a teenager with attitude and needs to be hitched in a specific order to maintain control. Once that was done, we got on the kamotiq. Each dog, with line taunt, eager to pull, was waiting for the sled to be released from the anchor. This is the time of greatest tension within the team. If the sled doesn't release right away, the dogs will usually attack one of their own, to release some of the tension that has built up. Luckily, we were off without a hitch, ha ha ha. Sorry I couldn't resist that one.

This time of year there is 4-5 inches of water on the ice, which made for a wet and wild time for the dogs and for us. Nonetheless, the dogs loved it and the water kept them cooled down. I was very much impressed at the way the lead dog obeys the commands of the operator. The commands are relatively simple, one set to go right and another set to go left. Every time the commands were given Rosie, the lead dog, changed direction. The whole dynamic of the team was something of beauty.

I thought I would give it a try and started with "Mush, mush doggies mush." They mostly ignored me except for the odd one that gave me glance as if to shut me up. I guess they didn't appreciate the humour at all. John told me that the expression is never used in the Arctic, but he did allude to the fact that it probably came about from a bad translation of one the Inuit commands. Well, the voyage down the Bay was underway, and we were all enjoying the day until........... How is that for tension. See you next week.

Mush Mush! - Part 2

The sun was at our backs and we were traveling down Frobisher Bay on a dog sled. What could possibly ruin the moment? Ok besides the fact that we could have fallen off the kamitiq and got soaking wet in the frigid water, or that we could have run into a huge crack in the sea-ice and perished in the icy waters below. Obviously that didn't happen. He he. The thing that put a sour taste in our mouths, literally, had to do with wind. Not the kind of wind that flies kites, and generates electricity, but wind of a different nature.

As we were enjoying the ride, all of a sudden the air took on a certain, pungent, flavour reminiscent of something rotten. It was the dogs, they were running their little hearts out, all the while breaking wind. dropping little surprises and whizzing. I never thought that the dogs would do that while they were pulling. Another lesson learned in the north. Kelly was wondering why I kept saying Rusty, until she remembered the Sienfeld Episode with Kramer driving the Hanson Cab after feeding the horse, Rusty, a mega sized beef-a-roni. Ha ha, Rusty.

The northern trade winds aside, the dogs were great. They were hitched in a fan formation (Inuit way) each with their own line. This method is used in Nunavut because of the lack of trees. Because each dog has their own line, they don't have to directly follow other dogs giving them more freedom. If this method was used below the tree line the dogs could get wrapped around one. We are so used to seeing dogs pulling sleds, like a stagecoach, as in the great races of the movies but this system works just as well. We went out past Tar Inlet then the lead dog, Rosie, was given the command to turn around and head home. We got back in one piece after a wonderful experience.

It takes a special kind of person to run a team of dogs.

They can't be tied up in town because of their aggressiveness. John was relating that if they had the opportunity, the dogs would finish him off. A nice, heart warming thought as he feeds them in the heart of the winter. A team of nine dogs needs about 60 seals to survive the winter and that can be hard to come by. The seals have to be cut up into milk crate size portions, and kept in a shed; which keeps them frozen. Two to three times a week one milk crate is thawed and delivered to the team. The day we went out was warm and sunny, very rare. The owners have to exercise the teams regardless of the temperatures. John has spent a lot of bitterly cold days with the team. Freezing his fingers hitching up in -60 degree weather, then going for a ride, and re-attaching them to the anchor. I remember the cold days of last winter and could not imagine, after working a long shift at work, coming home to a warm house only to turn around and battle the elements. John tells me that he knows the dogs are waiting for his arrival and he would feel so selfish and guilty that he wouldn't be able to sleep if he ignored them. I offered to hitch one of our cats to the front of the team to inspire and further motivate the team but Kelly would rather hitch me. I can only imagine that if I were hitched, there would be a lot more of the above-mentioned activities as I would be running in fear, and we know that bodily functions let loose from fear. I was only thinking of poor Dakota, our full-figured feline. I thought she might enjoy the exercise. I was wrong.

Polar Man

Every town has it's local characters. Pictou has many; and you know who you are. Iqaluit is no exception. If you're here for a week you can't miss our most famous character - Polarman.

I heard about him before I met him. Rumour has it he was in a car accident as a child and is developmentally delayed. I thought all the stories my co-workers told me about him were exaggerated. I mean, what grown man wears a mask, tights and a cape? I was involved in that one incident in Antigonish a few years back, the RCMP have it on file - but I digress. Could this man really think he is a superhero and if so what powers does he think he possesses?

It turns out Polarman, and make no mistake about it, Polarman is his name of choice, knows he has no superpowers. He does, however, wear his 'get up' every day. I don't know any-one who has seen him without the mask but I'm sure it does come off once in a while. He doesn't bath very often and near the end of winter, the smell can be overpowering.

His goal in life is to protect small children from bullies and keep our parks safe and clean. Also, to keep all driveways and walkways free of snow with his trusty shovel, for a nominal fee. (Polarman's services don't always come free!) I've gleaned this information from his sporadic letters to the editor of our weekly newspaper, Nunatsiaq News. He is sure to be found at any community event, and even has seasonal accoutrements for his costume. My favourite so far is Christmas. He adds caribou antlers to his headgear. I guess he's supposed to be a reindeer.

Doing some internet research on Nunavut last week, I stumbled across a site that not only mentions him but has an interview and photo. (www.joshuafoermeetstheworld.com for anyone who's interested). Incidentally, just before press time, I learned that Polarman also has his own website but I don't have the address. I was surprised to learn two previously unknown facts about Polarman: First, Polarman was introduced to the Queen of England on her short 2002 visit to Iqaluit (I would love to hear her thoughts on him) and second, Polarman was not always Polarman. He started off as Polarboy and graduated to the position of 'Man'. Apparently, it was quite a shing-dig up here.

This last point begs the question, does this leave room in the world for a new Polarboy? Qualifications would have to include enjoying children, pet rats, shoveling snow and talking A LOT! Did I mention that? Getting caught talking to Polarman when you're in a hurry is worse than getting stuck looking at Kelly's baby photos of her two cats! Anyone interested in applying, let me know. I can be reached at Barbara-Ann and Ira's for a couple of weeks - ah, sweet vacation! It doesn't pay well, there's no housing allowance available but you might meet the Queen!

A BumbleBee

I saw a bumblebee today. I didn't think that would ever please me as much as it does. I came outside to write as it's one of the first really nice days we've had. So far I've seen a bumblebee, a housefly and a mosquito.

At home in Nova Scotia, I always used to feel, that spring would never come. Well, let me tell you, we're four days away from the first day of summer and I just saw my first insects! The bay is still frozen but the surrounding land is mostly clear of snow. The small creeks are running free again. Did I mention it's almost summer? You learn not to take the nice days for granted.

The Rotary Club Park in Apex (5 minute drive from Iqaluit) seems like a little slice of heaven today. I'm in shirt sleeves, the bustle of Iqaluit is out of ear shot and children are scattered in the distance, roaming like ants among the hills and rocks. A tent is pitched on the next hill over. It could have been there all winter. Hard to tell as some people do leave them up. Still, it reminds me of camping and summer breezes.

Then I turn my head. There are people walking out on the sea ice. That's how strong and thick it still is. To be honest, until a few minutes ago I thought they might be caribou and I was getting kind of excited but I can see now that they're the two legged variety of creature. It's hard to reconcile the two views. Winter Wonderland in one corner and spring fever in the other.

When we get back from vacation, 'summer' will be in full swing. Not the 'spend the afternoon at Waterside beach and take in an outdoor concert at the waterfront marina in the evening' kind of summer but summer nonetheless. The Inuit people certainly take advantage of any and all weather that's anywhere above -20C. Even six weeks ago, on days when Pictou teenagers probably would be huddled in the Youth Center, avoiding the outdoors, youngsters here were in shirt-sleeves playing basketball across from Northmart. This summer I plan to follow the Inuit example and not waste my time indoors. Winter's long enough. With a little luck, this will be our last full summer here and I'm going to take it all in.

This of course, means I have only one summer left to redeem myself in my father-in-law's eyes. Yes, the elusive arctic char - I'm coming for you this year! Ira will rue the day he laughed at my fishing skills! (Evil laughter here). Well, maybe not, but I'd really, really like to catch one!

Epilogue: Two days after this was written, it snowed again. The MacInnis's happily packed for vacation and Robbie still hadn't caught a fish.

Carnival

Well it is over for another year. Lobster Carnival 2004 was a success as usual. Mind you, having been sheltered from the pre-carnival craziness by being away and also by having  only a limited amount of carnie experience to draw upon, my opinion might not count but let me tell you, my head and body tell me that it better have been a great time. I was fortunate enough to be able to play with a great group during the parade, a new band called Na Gaisgich (Gordon Young's pet project for a number of years). These players are really a neat bunch to be around. I look forward to playing again with them.

However, the real highlight of the vacation was being surrounded by family and friends. There were a lot of gatherings, bbq's, and monumental occasions of extreme honesty and hilarity that only family and old friends can share. One such moment in particular happened as Miss X (identity protected not to spare her any undue embarrassment but for my health and well-being) explained to others of her "Experimental Flatulence" earlier that morning. Ha ha, now this concept is something that is practiced by every living person on earth, but was just never formally identified. Experimental Flatulence is the practice of letting out the gas very briefly and clandestine in nature to properly assess if the fragrance will be neutral enough to let fly at full capacity in an enclosed area or if the release should be controlled in a more ventilated area away from small children and open flames. This was both appreciated and understood by all, regardless of the laughter. You were not the only one to practice the ancient art of E.F. either, from what I was told.

Times like that can never be duplicated in a strange land, albeit still in Canada. There are moments of comradeship and good times but nothing to the degree that only can be achieved at home. As mentioned above, the practice of E.F. would still be done but the closeness between the people would not warrant a briefing after the fact. The reality is that the majority of us Southerners are all basically in the same boat, away from what is near and dear to our hearts. Everyone is always trying to make connections to home when they meet new people. Growing up, we always made fun of people from New Waterford, as they did of people from Dominion, and so on. I have a friend now not only from New Waterford but one from East Bay as well. Unheard of I know, but still true. I still send some friendly fire their way but it is all taken in stride as we all bind ourselves together for the Maritime connection more than anything else.

Going back to Iqaluit, means leaving our families and friends once again; carrying a lot of luggage, and heavier hearts. But it has a positive side as well. It means that we are closer to the end of our commitment and return to home. Every cloud does have a silver lining. My return also puts me into fishing season, and my quest to land the char. Now I have some flies from Don MacLean which he boasts guarantee success. I might prove to be the best fisherman in the North yet. Ha ha right.

Next week, I will try to paint a picture for you of my night playing cards with George Falconer, Ira and Barbara-Ann. I think I uncovered their strategies of play.

Auction

Ah, what would life be like without Auction? Throughout northern Nova Scotia and Cape Breton there are nightly card games hosted by one organization or another. The stakes are never large but an evening of fun is almost a guarantee. I have found that the players strictly enforce the rules but the consistency in the rules varies from game to game. In the Arctic, there are neither games listed in the paper nor any indication of underground games. Ole Crackie never heard of the game but wondered if it was like Fish. I mentally envisioned the whole explanation process that would have to occur in order to tell him no, and settled on telling him that they were close.

I was first schooled in Auction while doing contracting work for Michelin. Wild Bill explained the complexities of the game during lunch and smoke breaks. Now everyone that knows Wild Bill understands that he has a wonderful grasp on the English language and is never at a loss for colorful expressions, especially when it come to apparent rookie mistakes. The ever popular leading trump when it is not needed always triggered a marriage of adjectives and verbs that really when taken literally are impossible to perform.

After my baptism by fire, so to speak, I started to really take to the game and looked for opportunities to play. When the opportunity came to join Ira and Barbara Ann at George Falconer's for an evening of Auction I happily agreed. (Kelly ditched me for an evening at Relics with friends.) Being in George's house was like a trip back in time for me. The atmosphere reminded me of when we visited my Uncle Diddle's house growing up. It was a pleasant and welcomed feeling. Ole fashion hospitality was in abundance, along with crackers and seafood spread. After a period of small talk we got down to the business at hand. Ira was my partner, leaving George and Barbara Ann teamed up. I can't seem to remember who won overall that evening making me believe that it wasn't me but I did observe a few things that were interesting.

It was amazing how Barbara Ann always asked, loud enough for the neighbors to hear (quite a good distance), what the score was before bidding when she was winning or holding a great hand, but never had to be reminded when she was losing. I believe she just loved to hear Ira say he was not winning. We all know about the not talking across table rule. Ira has clearly solved this dilemma by his wonderful whistling when he has a good hand. As far as George is concerned, lets just say that he never had any problem telling us when he was holding a good hand. So now that I have figured out the players and there habits, their should be some great games on my next visit. Providing they don't hire a hit man to rub me out after my telling all their friends about their tricks.

The Price of Business

When one lives in the Canadian Arctic, one has to concede to a number of inconveniences. The weekend getaways become virtually non-existent, the romantic midnight strolls along a boardwalk are to be forgotten and the Saturday trip to Wal-Mart, ha ha, forget it. But what happened in the last month has to even make me shake my head.

There is a certain financial institution in Iqaluit that has been in operation for quite a few years now. They built a strong clientele long before it was renamed Iqaluit from Frobisher Bay. They also recruited a great number of clients from other communities up-island based on their mission statement on corporate responsibility: "Building on a tradition of social accountability, we remain committed to being actively and generously involved with the communities we serve." Which, honestly, sounds pretty good to me and must have to others as well. Last month customers were greeted at the door, not by a person, but a sign on the doors reading "We're Closing... At the close of the business day on Friday, November 5, 2004, we'll be moving to our Pembroke main office branch, located at 41 Pembroke Street West, in Pembroke, Ontario." That was the official announcement.

Pembroke, where the *&^%$ is Pembroke. I am sure it is a very nice community but how convenient can that be. Now I fully understand that a bank that earned over $600 million from its operations in Canada in a three-month period is not in the business to lose money, but the branch in question did turn a profit, just not a big enough profit. Lets say that if it was a money drain, they can't move it to a smaller community hoping for profit, so it logically should be moved to the next place "convenient" which to me and a number of other people felt should have been Ottawa, the first stop on the way south. But no, soon, customers will have to fly three hours to Ottawa, and then travel to Pembroke just to see a financial officer about their mortgages, RRSP's and, hopefully, get access to their safety deposit box. That would be kind of like a bank in Pictou saying that they will be moving to, let us for argument sake forget about the three-hour flight, Yarmouth. Yeah imagine how that would go over.

At least if the bank had moved to Ottawa, people would have a reasonable chance to step inside the branch to see who is handling their hard earned, and it is hard earned, money. Oh well, I guess the price of doing business has just gone up considerably in the North for some people who appreciate the local, human touch. Especially from a business whose Community Vision is documented as: "We strive also to build trusted relationships with the communities where we do business." I'm sure the community of Pembroke is sleeping well with that knowledge. The reason for Pembroke was that it is where the respective branches of this bank report to now and it was felt that they would have a better understanding of the needs in the North.

Next week, our trip to the Pangnirtung Fiord and why Jimmie should be mayor....

Pangnirtung or Panniqtuuq?

Last weekend, for my Birthday, we headed to the Hamlet of Pangnirtung for two reasons. One, just to get out of here for a couple of days and two, to satisfy our curiosity. Everybody kept saying that you have to see Pang before you leave, "Ya gotta see Pang." If you don't pronounce it right it means nothing or so they told me. I thought whatever, but I soon learned that Iqaluit is to School of Fishes as Panniqtuuq, not Pangnirtung is to the place of many bull caribou. Pangnirtung doesn't mean anything. See, was that so hard? I guess if you are going to say it, you might as well say it right. I think that is why so many just refer to it as simply Pang. So with our bags packed and picnic baskets filled, we headed for the Yellow Submarine.

In the aftermath of 9/11, I thought all passengers and flights had to be secure, but apparently up-Island flights don't. Everyone just walked out of the airport and on the plane, no x-rays or body frisking. That is my favorite part. Seriously, after a 45 minute flight, we entered the fiord of Pang and were greeted

by incredible scenery. The community of Pang is over a century old. But the Inuit from the Cumberland Sound area would gather once a year before that for the great whale hunt and to trade their furs and tusks at the trading post HBC set up at the same time. Eventually there was a permanent blubber station built to process whale fat. (And yes, smarty-pants, I had my picture taken there) A long and sorted history followed including a disease that destroyed most of the dog teams, and with it, the traditional way on life. The governing body at the time forced all the Inuit to move permanently into the hamlet and it grew from there. The community today has a population of 1,200 and hunting and fishing are the main industries. Pang is also internationally renowned for contributions to the art world, prints and woven crafts mainly.

With a little pre-trip research, we found out that the price of meals and groceries in the hamlet makes Iqaluit look like a bargain basement. A can of pop costs a mere $3.00 while a chocolate bar is $1.79. Meals at the lodge are charged by the day at $65.00/person. Regardless of the prices - remember the picnic basket - the trip was well worth it. We toured the visitors center, the Auyuittuq National Park center, the Uqqurmuit Centre for Arts and Crafts, all the stores, drove in the one and only taxi in town, and watched the Sea-lift unload its precious cargo, best three hours spent in a long time.

We managed to hire an outfitter to boat us to the National Park on Sunday. If a picture is worth a thousand words, we have around 49 thousand from that ride. The one down side of the community was the lack of customer service we are accustomed to. The receptionist at the lodge was not there to check us in, and there was an incident with our luggage and missing keys. The cashier at the craft center couldn't give us our change because the receipt never came out. Ten minutes later, and many attempts with a calculator we had our change. The cashier at Northern also had troubles with giving change. I am quite sure that, either I had the unfortunate chance of meeting the only three people of limited IQ in town, or barring that, Jimmie should think of moving there. He would be worshiped for his customer service skills and change making abilities. Mayor would be only a matter of time.

Inukshuks and Lighthouses

How many times have we all seen the vignette about the injured Mountie hobbling around watching the Inuit build an Inukshuk? He's wondering why they would go through all the trouble of building one. Then a little girl translates what the elder is saying for him, "Now they will know we were here." A very romantic image but not necessarily the correct one.

Inukshuk's are traditional route markers first and foremost; the fact that they signify man's presence was only a secondary benefit. Throughout the tundra of the north there are no real recognizable landmarks to show travelers the path to follow, so the Inuit had to make these structures. Inukshuk (pronounced Eee-nook-shook) is the Inuit word meaning "In the image of man". Groups of stacked stones, usually in human form, have been used by the peoples of the North for thousands of years. Built along treeless horizons, these landmarks helped travelers navigate on land and water. They were also used to help the Inuit herd caribou.

These beacons of the North are now seen as indicators of past Inuit presence as the vignette portrays, as well as route markers. However, a third purpose has evolved as of late. Inukshuks have now been adapted as symbols of friendship, reminding us that today, as in yesteryear, we all depend on one another. The image of a man, built of stacked stones by another man in order to help others find their way equates to friendship between men. Much could be said about that concept and how it can transcend cultures.

Nova Scotia has just lost one of its own beacons that also represented a route marker, a presence of man, and friendship. The loss of the Pictou lighthouse due to fire was tragic. It will be missed by all. The lighthouse helped many a ship avoid mishap, thus instilling a sense of trust and friendship with each safe passage past her. Every effort should be made to restore the harbour to its former beauty. The harbour seems to look lonely without its landmark protector.

Lastly, my family just flew into town for a weeklong visit. It should be interesting to see how they react to the Nunavut way of doing things. Yukon Jon has graciously donated his apartment for the week in order to accommodate us. Lots to see and do, caribou spotting, fishing for char, sightseeing, and of course the introduction to Jimmie Crack Corn. My mother is really anxious to finally meet the man, the one and only, my right hand man, the legend of the QuickStops. Ha ha. At the very least she will believe he actually exists.

Operation Narwhal

This past week has seen a great deal of activity in and around the North. The Iqaluit hockey camp was being conducted at the Arctic Winter Games Arena. The 10th Annual Iqaluit Music Camp was taking place, bringing my family because my brother was an instructor. The biggest activity was, and is, Operation Narwhal being conducted by the Canadian Forces.

Operation Narwhal is the biggest military exercise conducted in the North in a long, long time. It is being conducted in both Iqaluit and Pang and will last until the end of the month. The exercise, which is to provide a strong military presence in the North, involves all elements of the Canadian Forces, Air, Navy, and Land, and the reserve element, Canadian Rangers. It is nice to see the military presence. The training will bring with it a greater understanding of the diverse environments that make up Canada, and the challenges in protecting its sovereignty.

But what is really interesting and doesn't seem to get much attention is the name, Operation Narwhal. Well, operation is self-explanatory, but narwhal may not be. The Narwhal is an

Arctic whale. It is represented on the Nunavut coat of arms, along with a caribou, much like the mythical royal unicorn and

17th-century representation of a North American native is on Nova Scotia's. Narwhal means "corpse whale" in Old Norse, probably because of the colour of its skin, which is blueish-grey with white blotches. What is really neat, though, about these whales, are their tusks.

All narwhals have two teeth in their upper jaw. After the first year of the male narwhal's life, its left tooth grows outward, spirally. This long, single tooth projects from its upper jaw and can grow to be 7-10 feet long. Tusks are usually twisted in a counterclockwise direction and have a hollow interior. There have been double-tusked narwhals either sighted or captured over the years, but the norm is a single tusk. The purpose of the tusk is uncertain; thought to be a magnificent jousting weapon in courtship and in dominance rivalry. While not used for hunting, it is also speculated that they are used to channel and amplify sonar pulses (which they emit).

From medieval times through the 17th century, the spectacular spiraling tusk that Vikings would bring back to Europe reinforced belief in the existence of the unicorn. Narwhal tusks can be bought but at a price, in the thousands of dollars. Yukon Jon has one that is close to 7 feet tall and is truly a treasure he will cherish. I do have a plan though; I believe that if I can get him gooned up enough, I can replace his with a mound of spiraling mashed potatoes, much like in Close Encounters. Well, he might not notice right away. It should be a good experiment on my mashed potato creativity and his powers of observation.

The Last Straw

Last week during a seemingly innocent lunch break; a life changing decision was reached. Let me paint a picture for you. I got up as usual, did my morning routine of showering, coffee, etc. I dressed in a nice pair of light beige khakis with a blue sweater. When I came home at noon to have lunch, a most embarrassing event occurred. The button on my pants burst off. Now I have joked quite a bit about gaining a large waist since my arrival but I mean, come on. I blew the button off my pants. That has to be a sign for change.

Now, I am not saying that everybody at work is nosy, or pays extremely close attention to what I wear, but if I started the morning off with beige pants and returned from lunch sporting a blue pair, someone would be bound to notice. Lets face it; people in the Arctic are no different than people in Pictou in that regard. So I had a couple of options to weigh within the hour. I could fix the button, but that would have required knowledge of both button sewing and where to find the necessary equipment to complete the task. Another option would be to change my pants and hope no one would draw particular attention to the change. But that scenario would require an explanation that wouldn't make me look like a Fatty McButterPants or a sloppy eater who can't seem to find his mouth without dropping food on himself. So I did what any self-respecting person would do. I took a stapler, stapled the pants closed and tightened my belt to the point of rendering myself unconscious whenever I bent over. As long as I didn't drop anything for the remainder of the day, I should be able to pull the caper off. Well done to me I thought, with a congratulatory pat on the back.

But the fact that I was starting to burst out of my clothes had a great impact. I could either adjust my wardrobe accordingly to the next size up, start wearing a muumuu (Sam Moon style), or start my diet. Unfortunately the selection of business casual Muumuu's is limited up North, so out goes my evening routine of chips and dip, ice cream, and chocolate bars. I am pondering the possibility of actually exercising, but I am not going to jump on that bandwagon too quickly. Instead I'll wait on the results of my snack less diet for a month.

If the 2004 Olympics has shown the world, and me, anything, it is what fitness and determination can accomplish. They have, without a doubt, inspired many people to exercise and rejuvenate themselves. I am, all injuries and physical limitations aside, just plain too lazy to exercise. I know I lack the commitment required for a sculpted body. I need, want and demand instant results. If I do sit-ups I want to see noticeable results right away. So the thought of actual exercise is what I am calling Plan B. I realize that it is too late for this year, but as the summer starts to wind down, and Labor Day looms on the horizon, I would like people to not think that I could actually go into labour on that day. Ha ha, Burp, ha ha ha.

What Does That Mean, Really?

Moments after stepping off the plane in Iqaluit, Prime Minister Paul Martin declared, "I love the North." He went on to state "The North is an important part of what defines us as Canadians..." Hold on a minute, what does that mean exactly. Lets have a quick look at this shall we.

The notion of Canada being a northern country is a long-standing one, but a lot of people wonder what the real difference is between Canadians and Americans. The most simplistic response often imagined, I believe, would be the idea of a romantic, adventurous hinterland where man pitted against nature defines our strength. A nice thought, but a bit antiquated to say the least. By taking a look back at our own recent history, we as Canadians collectively have a difficult time trying to figure out what binds us together, except for maybe the proud and undeniable fact that we aren't American. So why does the image of an untainted wilderness not hold true you ask?

Well, the truth of the matter is that the majority of Canadians live in cities and the suburbs, most of which cast their shadows on the United States. There is an abundance of concrete, pollution and money within these communities. Nothing that resembles the wilderness so often envisioned. Even after five years, there are quite a few Canadians that couldn't tell you where the Hinterland, named Nunavut, is located on a map. Case in point would be that one major bank in Canada, not RBC, is unable to print cheques with Nunavut on the address.

Canada has been ranked the No. 1 Country in the world on a number of occasions because, generally speaking, we have a relatively low unemployment rate, a low crime rate on average, and manageable social problems. But having lived here over a year, I realize the North is a place of poverty, high crime, and seemingly unmanageable social problems. The amount of violent crime is off the chart and suicides are an all too common occurrence. Living in the modern North is not the romantic, untainted, wonderland that it used to be. It is a struggle, not against nature, but rather the all to common flaws of government. All three tiers of government have to take responsibility, but as usual, they spend precious time blaming each other.

After taking all this into account, what exactly is the important part that we contribute to our national identity as Canadians that the Prime Minister and other politicians have proclaimed. I realize that they are mostly blowing smoke up our derrières, because they honestly believe that is what we all want to hear. They are not entirely wrong to believe that. Human nature wants us all to believe we all are integral to the social fabric of our country; but seriously folks, the north is so far away from the majority of what makes Canadians Canadian. Oh well, on the bright side, maybe the next federal budget will reflect the importance and we will put an end to the poverty, and high crime rate, and try to put the social woes in a more manageable spectrum. Yeah right!!

Cape Dorset Carvings

Crafts are the pride and lifeblood of communities in every corner in the world. In Pictou, all one has to do is go for a stroll down Water Street and you will understand how much money is involved and how much is dependent upon these cottage industries. From rug-hooking, stained glass, to tole-painting and a multitude of others, there seems to be no end to the creativity that people possess. Some crafts stand the test of time while others make their mark and fade into the night; remember the faces made with dried up apples, and the lobster shell figurines.

Hanging in the halls of the Nunavut Legislative building is a rug hooking of the Nunavut Coat of Arms that was made in Cheticamp. The rug was Nova Scotia's gift to the newly formed territory. In November, John Bell Chapel, a private school's church, in Oakville, Ontario, will unveil a beautiful stained glass window crafted by Nova Scotian artisans. This stained glass was converted from a drawing by Cape Dorset artist, Kenojuak Ashevak. So it seems that Nova Scotia craftspeople are in demand abroad as well as at home.

In the North, as in Nova Scotia, many communities seem to be renowned for one unique craft. Pangnirtung for its woven hats, and prints, Cape Dorset for its carvings, etc, etc. Iqaluit is not celebrated for any one particular craft but does offer everything the other communities are famous for. When my family was up, we all went to the Frobisher Restaurant to sample the country foods of the north. As we ate, crafter after crafter approached the table to offer their wares. There were carvings ranging from $5 to over $1000, prints, fur and woven clothes, and jewelry. A lot of crafts entered the restaurant but few left with their creators, including the $1000 pieces.

Some crafters are quick to point out that they are not the

artist but are selling for a renowned artist, which drives the price up, whether it is true or not. Carvings in Cape Dorset fetch more money than anywhere else in the Arctic, so many sellers play upon this. Some have even sent their carvings from Iqaluit to Cape Dorset, via relatives already making the journey, to be sold for a higher price. Buyer beware is always the best bet.

Myself, I never have to worry about buying anything fraudulent in that regard. Why, you ask? It is because I only have a 6" by 4" piece of the apartment that I can decorate to my own taste. Hard as it is to believe, it is now filled. I think it would take an act of Parliament to get Kelly to relinquish more space for me. It seems that whatever carving I would find interesting or decorative is something she would describe as simply crap. So that's what they mean about having the upper hand.

The Terry Fox Run

For nearly a quarter of a century, thousands of Canadians have turned to their families and friends at this time of year, with pledge sheets, asking them to sponsor them in the Terry Fox Run. After which, they all turn out and enthusiastically endure the Run for Cancer. This event requires no further explanations from me, except that after 23 years of not participating, I finally did.

What changed my mind? Well I certainly didn't wake up that morning intending to do The Run. I can tell you that in all honesty. Not that I have anything against the program, I think it is a great legacy to the memory of a Canadian icon and his dream. I have sponsored a lot of participants in the past, up to and including this year. Kelly decided she was doing The Run, thus I sponsored her. But the thought of actually physically doing The Run has never appealed to me. I am more of a philanthropist than a participant. I always felt more comfortable putting my money where other people's mouths are. The thought of getting all those pledges and possibly not being able to finish just seemed wrong to me. Would I have to give the money back? What if I only completed half, would I be required to return half the pledge money? What would I tell them? "Hey there Jimmie. I guess since you pledged $10.00 and I only got half way around the route before collapsing into a quivering ball of sweat and exhaustion, I owe you $5.00. I only hope they aren't $5.00 short on finding a breakthrough. Eeeeep!!!!!" As you can see, there were more reasons than just being out of shape.

So, why did I change my mind? Well, the day of The Run, Kelly's co-worker called and backed out which left Kelly going it alone. Since I had already decided I was going to go do some administration work for cadets while she did her walk, I didn't think much about it. She left about 15 minutes before me, but I had to pass the starting line to get to where I was going. As I got closer to the crowd, I could see her standing there in the cold as it started to drizzle. She smiled and waved as I drove by. There was something about her standing there, alone amongst the crowd; with her Dal hat and yellow jacket that stopped me pretty much in my tracks. I decided that my place to be on this miserable day was next to her as she walked the route to unselfishly help others.

What I didn't realize, however, is that she wasn't completely alone. She had met up with the new physiotherapist, and had just finished telling her there goes her lazy husband just driving by. Oh well, it was true. She was really surprised when I showed up, supporting her in what she was doing. I've got to say, that has to be a big checkmark for me in the big guys book upstairs. Regardless of that, The Terry Fox Run had done more than make money today. It has brought strangers closer together, and more importantly, it has shown me once again that I married the right girl. And I guess the exercise was a good thing too…

Silent Givers

The next time you are at work or your local volunteer activity, there is one thing you can look for and may, or may not, find. That is the person who takes credit for everything. Well, not necessarily everything but you know the type of person I'm referring to. They are the ones who seem to know everything about the organization even though they might have just joined the group. They almost never take advice from people who have experience, doing things their own way instead. They have a certain way of showing up when photographs are being taken and often seek praise from others, including self-praise for that matter.

The silver lining to this cloud is there are a lot of volunteers who prefer to give up their time without recognition at all. These are the people who have chameleon-like characteristics that make them fade into the background. They shy away from the limelight whenever possible and hesitantly accept praise with embarrassment and humility, but appreciate it deep down when they are recognized. These are the people, I am proud to say, that make up the majority of Maritimers.

I had the pleasure of having my fair share of working along side both. While I think that the former has many obnoxious traits, they can be vital to providing a much-needed voice to their respective programs or charities. I have a great deal more respect for those I like to call the 'Silent Givers'. They are the backbone and life-blood of any organization. Which group would I fit into? Well, I seem to be outspoken, as well as possessing a "full of myself" quality toward many things (or so I am told, ha ha). That having been said, I think I am a silent giver. My friends should back me up on this one, I hope, saying that I never look for praise, often ensuring that the praise be focused elsewhere. I believe the reward of seeing the positive results at the end is enough.

I am involved presently, with a non-silent giver and it is frustrating to deal with him at times. During a meeting with this non-silent giver, not a word of lie, we had a lengthy debate over what date Victoria Day landed on. He had a calendar, but it didn't list holidays, while I had a calendar, in my hand, which clearly and unequivically showed the date. He went on and on about how he was right and the calendar was obviously wrong. Even after checking another calendar, he still didn't admit defeat changing the subject instead. As Bugs Bunny would say, "What a Maroon!" He always has to identify himself, publicly, as the boss and clearly loves to hear himself talk whenever there is an audience. He is not from the Maritimes, but is lucky enough to have enough silent givers on the team to make sure at the end of the day everything gets completed and the goals are met

The moral of this whole rant is that growing up in Nova Scotia has given me the confidence to stand up for what is right, logically and/or morally, and to give freely of my time to help the community better itself. Most of us, having been brought up in tight knit communities, either in Cape Breton or Pictou County, inherited a sense of ownership to our surroundings, and feel the same sense of responsibility. Since moving here, I still have that dedication to help out but can't help noticing the reality of the difference between Maritimers and the rest, Silent Givers and the non-Silent Givers.

Technology

I never really paid that close attention to the little changes that happen in the world but when I recently stopped and reflected back, wow. I, like most people in Nova Scotia, grew up in a warm, loving but financially modest home. There usually wasn't enough money for the latest technological gismo on the market. Computers were not part of my education until I started my undergraduate degree in the latter part of the 80's. One of the prerequisite courses was to take computers. At the time, we were learning to use Basic, Cobol, and Fortran languages, two of which I still don't know what the H*&$ they are. There was no such contraption as a compact disc, and the floppy discs we used were actually, well, floppy. Email was a thing of the future and the internet still didn't exist. How things have changed, and how silently they have changed our way of life.

Today I sit here, in front of a laptop computer, using a window based, user friendly, operating system to type this column. When I finish, I will check the spelling, grammar, and if necessary, move entire paragraphs around with a click of a mouse. I frequently use the internet to research and will eventually send this finished product to Pictou over the internet, via phone lines, satellites and fiber optics. In actuality, in the year and some since I started appearing here, I have never met the editor, or anyone else from the Advocate for that matter. In fairness, he has graciously offered to meet on several occasions but I declined as time was always compressed.

Changes in technology have made it entirely possible for me to still be part of a community while I am physically absent. Every Saturday, I enjoy my Pictou County hour; I listen to CKEC over the web, check into the Pictou website for news, photos and the guest book while reading my copy of the Advocate and Cape Breton Post. Listening to the familiar voices, the commercials, while browsing the newspapers, seems to take me out of the Arctic and back in my living room at home in Nova Scotia even if only for an hour a week. An hour a week in Pictou is better than a month in Iqaluit for me.

Some people move here and love it, but I am not one of them. Not because I hate it here but because I would rather be home-plain and simple. Last week while you guys seemed to enjoy warm, autumn weather, it snowed four out of seven days; two being near blizzard conditions. It is still September. Since we arrived last year, a number of people have asked us about the living conditions. Well, if you don't mind cold weather and snow 10 months a year, or being confined to one community for long periods of time, then this could be the place for you. There is a lot of work in a multitude of job sectors, the money is fantastic and for the outdoor enthusiast there's an endless amount of terrain for ATV's and snowmobiles. For those more skilled than me, hunting, and fishing seems to be a big draw as well.

Last but not least, thankfully, the technology that has slowly but surely entered our lives means I can talk to someone back home instantly while seeing them through a web cam. Pictures can be sent within seconds making the sharing of special moments possible. Technology still has its drawbacks however, I still can't get a slice of Pictou County pizza late at night....he he he!!!

Thanksgiving Day

Thanksgiving Day in Iqaluit, now there is something they won't be writing songs about anytime soon. Besides the obvious lack of free-range turkeys running about, garden fresh vegetables, or anything else that seems to be relative to the traditional harvesting celebration held in the homes throughout Pictou County, there is a commercial value that is missing as well. Singing lyrics like;"Chewing Muktuk by an open ice hole" (to the tune of chestnuts roasting on a open fire) just doesn't conjure up the same warm feeling or visions. I can't help but think that the concept of celebrating Thanksgiving Day, as we know it, was a southern import.

The Arctic can, however, claim to have a distinct connection to the holiday, albeit a vague one. After one of his early voyages to Canada, on May 27, 1578, English navigator Martin Frobisher held a ceremony in what is now called the province of Newfoundland and Labrador to give thanks for surviving his journey. This occurred forty-three years before the Pilgrims' celebrations at Plymouth Rock, in 1621. This is considered one of the first thanksgivings in North America. Seeing how Iqaluit sits on the shores of Frobisher Bay and was once named Frobisher Bay, that is how the connection is made. Well, I told you it was vague.

Having said all that, this will be my second Turkey Day spent north of the 60th parallel and I truly do have something to be thankful about this year. It will be my last north of sixty. Don't get me wrong, I am thankful for my family and friends, their collective good health, and the opportunities that have afforded me the life I live, but holidays always make me long for home.

This year we will be having the dinner at a friend's home and for two really good reasons. One, to spend the holiday amongst others so we won't look like losers, and two, it is really difficult to find a frozen turkey for two people. Why should we, or would we, bother spending all that time thawing, cleaning, stuffing, and basting a bird that would feed a small army when it is just the two of us. It just doesn't make sense. Sure we could have a chicken, but that sounds too everydayish. Cornish hen, too pretentious (not to mention that I wouldn't know where to start cooking it. What would I baste it with an eyedropper), Duck and goose, too difficult to find. See my problem. Although, really when I think about it, next year won't be much different. I will be still leeching a free turkey dinner; only it will be at Ira and Barbara-Ann's. I only hope Ira won't be as cheap with the stuffing as this years host, who absent-mindedly kept it in the oven until after the meal was over. For me, being a guy who doesn't eat any fruits or vegetables, I rely on a good dressing or stuffing for the meal. In reality, nothing could say Thanksgiving better than Stove-Top Stuffing to cleanse the palate between the entrée and dessert.

Bad Service or No Service

I want you to stop and think for a brief moment about how you would rate the service industry in Pictou County. Think about an example of good service that you received and another example of bad service. I can almost guarantee that you have thought of at least two or three bad examples before a good example popped into mind. The reason is most people tend to remember bad customer service more than good customer service. Following that line of reasoning, I should remember every shopping experience I had up here, he he.

I have always considered myself very even-tempered and take a lot of things in stride, but last week really took the cake. Living in Nova Scotia, I had gotten used to being in a competitive market and the quality of service that dictates. If I made an appointment at a garage to have my car looked at I realized that it wouldn't be cheap but at least the service I received ensured my vehicle was fixed in a reasonable time frame, usually with a guarantee that the job was done right. Weeks ago, we called the garage up here and told them EXACTLY what we wanted done so they could have the necessary parts on hand and made an appointment for the following week. I took the truck to the garage at 8:30 am, explained again, not to the service writer, but to the automotive repair technician (see I can be PC if I want, ha ha) himself, what I wanted to see happen. I wanted the driver's side front tire replaced, the heater blower motor replaced, the oil changed and the coolant checked. I returned at the end of the workday to pick up the truck and pay for the damages.

When I got there, the same guy gave me my keys back while explaining that I needed to replace the driver's side front tire, the blower motor was also broke and needed to be replaced. He then explained that he changed the oil and checked the coolant, which was fine. Then he passed me the bill for $140 plus change. Holy $%^!!!! $140 to change the oil and tell me what I told him 8 hours earlier. I realize that the shop charges are $100/hr here but seriously, don't charge me for what I already told you. That is just not right, I mean, I didn't even get a kiss before the bill, if you get my drift. It is now two weeks later and I still haven't got the blower motor replaced because they didn't realize, after being told three times to order the motor, that they had to order the motor.

This kind of service is the norm in the North, and you have to just learn to accept it. It is either bad customer service or no customer service. The lack of competition means that they really have nothing to worry about. They either do the work or nobody does it. So the next time you go to the garage or any-where else for that matter, appreciate the service you are receiv-ing. It could be a lot worse. I know.

Traffic Jams Northern Style

A traffic jam is probably the most annoying man-made occurrence we as a society have come up with in the last century. They never occur at a good time for anybody and they are never soothing or easy on the nerves. But I can guarantee you one thing about them; if you are in a hurry, you are certain to run into one. On the bright side, it is one way to keep high-blood pressure medication selling, and that is job security for the pharmaceutical industry.

Outside of festivals and special events, Pictou normally has traffic flow problems at the Sobey's entrance and at the three way stop by Needs, from what I remember. Huh, now when I write it like that it sounds like I am implying that the Sobey's empire has created them, but it is just a coincidence I am certain. (Or am I,) But we all have learned to deal with them, and in some ways to avoid them. That is exactly what I thought we were doing when we left - avoiding them. We didn't purposely move to Canada's frozen tundra capital to specifically avoid the traffic jams of Pictou County, but I thought that the North would offer me a few scrap of hope to cling to. You know, the not having to mow the lawn, rake the leaves, or never getting caught in a traffic jam kind of scrap that would throw a positive spin on things.

Never before have I seen a traffic jam in any footage of the North, nothing was ever said to us about this possibility before we moved. In actuality, we were told quite the opposite, that there were not a lot of cars in the North and that most people didn't have one. They were right on the money about both, truth be told. The total number of vehicles "registered" in Nunavut stands at 3000, and that according to the Registry of Motor Vehicles equates to approximately 99 vehicles per 1000 people. The North West Territories stands at around 415 per 1000 in contrast.

What those statistics don't say is that the majority of those vehicles are located in one place in Nunavut. That is a fair number of vehicles for a city with limited roads and parking. This sealift season alone has seen roughly 200 more vehicles arrive to the capital city, with another 40 going up-island. What does that means for us? Well, another 200 cars trying to compete for limited parking and that peak traffic times are more congested than last year creating up to a 10 minute wait at intersections. It also means the possibility of a gas shortage before the spring breakup, like what happened in Pangnirtung last spring. They had to fly it in daily and ration it out. There is also the problem of no recycling program in place for the junk vehicles.

So next time you find yourself stuck in traffic, think about poor, lil' me sitting in a 10 minute traffic jam in the Arctic, with no Tim's, stuck between Betty Two Skidoos, Yukon Jon, and Jimmie trying to get to work which I could quite conceivably walk faster to if I wanted, but won't, because that would be exercise and we both know my stance on that.

Circle Check

One of the requirements that the Military has when taking one of their vehicles out is to always do a circle check around the vehicle before you move it. This is to ensure that there is nothing visibly wrong such as a flat tire or broken light. Pilots have to do a more thorough check around their aircraft, which makes sense. Even when you rent a vehicle from Enterprise, Hertz or wherever, they walk you around the car to check for damage, dents, and scratches. Having such training, you would think that I would be in the habit of doing a circle check every time I go anywhere. Oh, but no, that would be too smart for me. I always have to learn things the hard way .

On Thursday, I had the parking space closest to the road at the bank, which means that I would just hop in at the end of the day and pull away to go home. Which is exactly what I did. The traffic was normal for that time of day, not bumper to bumper, but just enough to never get out of 2nd gear. The speed limit is only 30km/hour.

As I was driving home though, I noticed that there were a lot of people being overly friendly, or so I thought at the time. They were kind of looking at the truck and "waving", which was strange because I normally only meet one or two people that I know well enough to exchange salutations. It wasn't until I got home that I realized the reason. Some crazy person had tied their husky to my bumper while they went into the bank machine. So as I drove home, the dog was running behind the truck, I couldn't see him in the rearview mirror because he was tied up short enough to block it, but long enough to give him enough lead to run without hindrance.

The dog was fine, unharmed, and friendly after the unexpected run. He seemed to have actually enjoyed it. Now before you get all upset about this, I too was equally horrified at the discovery. I returned the dog, inside the truck this time, to his much embarrassed and worried owner. He was really thankful the dog wasn't harmed, explained that that was the first time anything like that has happened to him. He vowed never to hitch his pet to the bumper of another vehicle.

It sounds a lot like National Lampoons Summer Vacation with Chevy Chase portraying the bumbling Clark Griswold, but in my case, the dog was fine. Living in the Arctic, one gets used to things that you would never see in Pictou; like finding a person shopping for groceries with a rifle strapped to his back, or people taking a dog team and Kamatiq to church. But it happens and just because no one in Pictou ties their animals to a bumper as they run errands doesn't mean it couldn't happen. The moral of the story is two fold. One, never tie your pet to a strange vehicle's bumper, and two, try to circle your vehicle every time you get in. You just never know what could be tied to it or hiding under it. An ounce of prevention is better than a pound of cure. I can picture my mother now, standing with one hand on her hip and the other hand shaking her pointed finger at me as she starts it off with "Now Robbie, an ounce..." and maybe someday it will sink in. I doubt it.

Passwords, Friends or Foe

Whether we like it or not, we are living in a world dependant upon a multitude of passwords. They have been around for a lot longer than most people realize. My earliest memories of passwords, were the secret passwords used on Sesame Street to open doors or other things. "Open Sesame" was one, and "A La Peanut Butter Sandwiches" was the other one. I always preferred the latter because it sounded funnier rolling off the tongue and I could employ a sense of drama if needed. Since then, however, I seemed to have added one after the other, so much so, that it has gotten out of control. I now have a password to remember my passwords. Sadly though, I am serious.

Just stop for a second, and think about how many you have. Credit cards and bank cards have PIN numbers to access ATM's. Email accounts, alarm systems, keyless entry systems on vehicles all have them, and the list goes on and on. I have so many that I actually had to store them in a computer file, password protected of course, in order to remember them all.

On any given day, I need up to five different passwords at work in order to do my job. I have bank accounts at two different institutions, both with cards with PIN numbers and internet banking with completely different passwords. In order to function at cadets, I need one for the building alarm and two for the computer in order to log on, plus two more for access to related national websites to do my work. At home, I need more passwords to access our answering machine, the laptop computer and email. I used to have another set of passwords for the Quickie Mart, but thankfully, I can forget them now. So why not use the same one for everything? Because some have to be alphanumerical, some are just numerical, and some that have to be upper and lower case sensitive. So as you can see, I really don't see an end to them anytime soon.

In an electronic age, however, they are extremely important, to protect us against fraud, such as Identity Theft; a popular crime the last couple of years, and one that is being battled
against everyday. But seriously, there has to be a better way on
the horizon.

In the meantime, I have recently stopped to think about
how would I feel if someone stole my identity. It would be
unsettling and extremely frustrating trying to regain it, dealing
with the legalities of financial responsibility and such. Maybe it
wouldn't be totally bad in a way. If in the process of stealing my
identity, they paid my debts, dealt with Kelly when she was
upset at me, exercised for me, brushed the cats, cleaned the
oven, and took out the garbage, it might be worth the aggrava-
tion. Obviously I am kidding about the exercise, I wouldn't wish
that on anyone, not even the fraudulent me……

The DEW Line

I am going to start with a brief history lesson, but bear with me, I am going somewhere with this. (I hope so anyway.) Fifty years ago, Canada and the United States approved the construction of the Distant Early Warning Line. This consisted of 58 sites, known as the DEW line, strung from Alaska to Greenland along the 68th parallel, and intended to serve as a radar shield to detect Soviet bombers.

The DEW line would act as the primary air defense warning during an "Over-the-Pole" invasion of North America. Pretty fascinating stuff, eh.

But, by the time the DEW line was completed in 1957, it was already obsolete. The line offered no guarantees that any enemy bombers could or would be shot down; however, it did act as an effective deterrent until the unmanned North Warning System replaced it in the 80's. Sounds like typical government work, doesn't it, going ahead and completing a project just in time for it to be obsolete.

Now to my point, people say that time will heal all wounds but the construction of the DEW line was such an extreme upheaval to the Inuit way of life, one that dealt a wound that will never be healed in their eyes. Before the DEW line arrived, the proposed sites were a quiet part of the world, except for the wind. That all changed when the project was approved. That meant there were now 120 ships in two convoys delivering 23,000 construction workers, 42,000 tonnes of steel, hundreds of million litres of fuel to the Arctic, to places that had never seen so much as a building before.

Naturally the Inuit were intrigued by all the commotion, and many were hired to help. The housing, money and medical attention was well received but with it, they lost a piece of their past. People were encouraged to move into communities, and suddenly there was urbanization that never existed before.

The DEW line had a positive impact as well. For one thing, the line opened up air transportation in the Arctic. As a result, it was ultimately responsible for the development of cooperatives because it made the transportation logistics possible. Did the positive impacts out weigh the bad? I think so, but that is just my humble opinion.

Many Inuit still get sentimental about the old way of life before the DEW line and are quick to criticize the forces of change, but ironically do so surrounded by the comforts of their new way of life. Go figure. They are not unlike other cultures, in expressing their desire for the simpler way of life their ancestors lived. People, let us all be honest with ourselves. If we are not happy with the way our lives are lived now, why do we constantly upgrade our lifestyles with the newest and latest instead of gravitating towards the olden ways we romanticize about. Why don't these people who complain, just go ahead and do it. I'll tell you why. Because we all truly realize and respect the hardships that our ancestors had to endure and wouldn't trade the comforts of our modern lives to live that way again. That is what camping is for, roughing it for a couple of days to make us realize how good we have it. I know I would rather be in my house in Pictou, than in damp, sod house in the moors of Scotland for the rest of my life. But hey, that's just me......

Christmas Vacations

This is the time of year when everyone living away from home starts to make plans for Christmas and vacations. The talk around the North for the last two weeks was all about departure and return dates. With such a transient society up here, if anyone wants to travel home for the holidays, they have to book well in advance. Working at the bank, I talk to a lot of people who are either traveling home or punching Deep South for a well-deserved break from the icy climate.

Last Christmas, Kelly's best friend and fellow ex-patriot Pictonian living in Calgary, Nadine LeBlanc gave her a novel by John Grisham entitled Skipping Christmas. The story starts with a married couple seeing their only child move away with the Peace Corps for a two-year stint (kind of paralleling us in a way). Since this will be the first Christmas without her, they decide to plan a cruise and skip the entire holiday hustle and bustle. The story has its comical aspects about the expectations, traditional rituals and responsibilities we all go through during the holidays, Their escape to the sun takes a disastrous turn when their daughter calls the day before they leave, Christmas Eve, and tells them she is on the way home that day. The book was turned into a motion picture that is in theatres as we speak, Christmas with the Kranks.

We missed the holiday season last year, and sadly we won't be able to be there again this year. We did get home in January and all our friends and families graciously left their homes decorated for us, a gesture we will never forget. It was belated, but it was really nice to be able to celebrate the season Nova Scotia style.

After reading the book and seeing the trailers for the movie, I couldn't help but think about what would happen if we decided to arrive home just before Ira and Barbara-Ann were to leave on a cruise. Without spoiling either the book or movie for anyone, I can see Ira hastily stringing lights on his many deer heads, Barbara-Ann running around the house decorating, desperately searching for Father Pigmus (a favorite of Kelly and Nadine) with the dogs chasing her from room to room.

I can also see my family scrambling to prepare for our unscheduled arrival. But alas, with our work schedules it is not possible.

So after a quick budget adjustment, we booked tickets and are arriving at Halifax Airport this Saturday, yes that's right the 27 Nov, for a quick four-day whirlwind pre-Christmas visit. Surprise!! Seeing how we told nobody, I really hope Ira, Barbara-Ann, Joyce or Danny actually do read this column every week like they tell me, because we need a lift from the airport at 9:30 am. If not, I guess we will be mirroring another movie for four days, The Terminal.

We both look forward to seeing everyone soon, and to my buddy Linda, at Ahead of Hair, I need a haircut so book me in.

Travel

Traveling can be stressful for the best of people, but when you make travel arrangements in the North, you have to have either nerves of steel, or a come-what-may attitude. Thursday night we checked with Enviroment Canada for the weather forecast and they were calling for a blizzard on Friday, starting in the afternoon. Now, we had booked the 6:10 pm flight out of Iqaluit, so a blizzard would essential destroy everything we planned.

Friday morning arrived with clear skies, and we both went to work on pins and needles for the rest of the day. The buzz all around town was about the blizzard; when it will hit, how long it will last, and how much precious snow it will leave behind. I can't speak for Kelly but my day consisted mainly of two separate conversations with everybody. I would be polite with everybody who commented on the blizzard, "Oh my Stars, yes dear, indeed a good blizzard would be nice for the snow machines." But in my head, I was saying "Listen you old Battle-Axe, I have a #$%^ flight to catch today, and don't particularly enjoy your positive attitude about getting a storm, so why don't you shut your MukTuk hole until I leave, then you can have your precious blizzard." Ha ha ha, As the plane was taking off, the talk was of the blizzard hitting around midnight and lasting until Sunday. I didn't care, because I was on my way home to familiar surroundings, and to everything I was sure of.

As for familiar surroundings, I found out when I got home to Pictou County that I haven't mastered all the skills required to be a true Pictonian. This was until Saturday evening when I witnessed and was part of, an entire conversation about Pictou county travel

and about going "in town", "up town", or "over town". To make matters worse, apparently depending on your starting point, these words have different end points.

From Three Brooks, "in town" is Pictou and "up town" is New Glasgow. But from, lets say the Parkers in West River, "in town" means New Glasgow. To throw more flies in the ointment, some of the older generation, those who had a lot of Gaelic spoken around them, still refer to Antigonish as the Big Town and New Glasgow as the Small Town. Can you see now, how a poor Cape Bretoner like me would be like a fish out of water.

I can picture everyone now, thinking what an idiot I would look like going "in town" to shop at Wally World, standing there scratching my head, when clearly everyone knows that Wally World is "up town" in the Highland Square. I guess I still have a lot to learn about being a Pictou County Boy, but thankfully I have many good people to set me straight. Ha ha ha.

Holiday Stress

The holidays can be a time of great stress for many people. There always seems to be more that has to be accomplished than time allowed for it to be done. Christmas concerts for the various organizations we belong to fill at least 4-5 evenings in December. Shopping for that perfect gift will take up a good, solid week in total. A parade always takes up an afternoon, and it is not like we can expect a surprise ending. Every one of us stands in the cold waiting for a jolly, fat man in a red suit to end the parade, and low and behold, he always does. I think I will skip the parade next year, instead I will just put on a red sweater and look in the mirror, fill my face with chocolate and candy canes until I get sick. At least I'll be warm. Ha ha

And let us not forget about the stress and agony of trying to find just the right thing to write on the numerous cards we send. Since most cards already include Merry Christmas and a Happy New Year, we all find ourselves compelled to babble on in addition to the greeting because it would just seem so impersonal not to. A few years back, I spent an entire day writing cards, to eventually realize that I started to tell a story on one card and finished the story on the last card. Every one I knew was told a small part of my year, but nobody the entire story. This year, we decided to write the "up-until-now, dorky, but-not-now, because-we-are-doing-it" Christmas letter and stuffed the cards with them. Man, I am really starting to be domesticated. I should just throw in the towel, and buy a minivan or station wagon. Of course, it would have to have "Sport" embossed somewhere near the name just to appease my fleeting sense of manhood.

Staff parties are always good for stress relief for me though. Although the secret Santa gift exchange can cause ulcers in some self-conscious people. Did I spend enough? Maybe I spent too much. What if my gift is better than what I gave? What if they don't like it? And how far can you take a gag gift without crossing the line?

Then there is the matter of what to wear. The questions that women ask us. Is this frock too trampish, or does it make my butt look big? If there is a right answer for those old chestnuts of the season, I wish someone would tell me. And if the party is at a staff member's home, should I bring something even though they said not to bother?

Office parties are also a great opportunity to witness exceptional social skills normaly not seen. If you looked up staff party in an illustrated dictionary, I am quite sure you will find a picture of people standing around drinking, sitting on desks or furniture, and one person in the background wearing a lampshade or photocopying their rear-end. I always seem to have the ability to find myself attached to that person. I am like a lighthouse to the drunkest, most opinionated person in the room. You know the type I am talking about. The ones that have to hold your arm as they tell you the most fascinating stories the world has ever known, loud enough for everyone in the room to hear. This always impresses Kelly to no end. Knowing how much she is impressed with me and the situation that I have surrounded myself with; that really takes the holiday stress away from me.

So as you can see, even though I am thousands of miles away from family and friends, the stress of holidays is still present, but thanks to staff parties, my stress level never gets out of control. Ha ha!

Santa Claus

When I was a young lad in Cape Breton, there was no one who believed in Santa Claus more than me. The whole frenzy around Santa used to start when the Eaton's and Simpson-Sears Catalogues hit the mailbox in October. My brother, sister and me, would fight over who would get the first peek inside the wonderful book from Santa, thinking it was from him, of course.(at least that was my perception) My mother used to tell us to circle what we wanted Santa to bring us. Looking back, he was pretty accurate delivering us the loot, er, presents.

When we got older, the Consumer's Distributing Catalogue replaced the Eaton's catalogue. This one was always a favorite, I think because of the glossy paper and brighter pictures. Everything always looked better in there. It was around then that the ritual changed. My mother gave us a price range and we had to decide what we wanted within that price range. So with those parameters prescribed, we would spend countless hours pouring over the books, no longer circling but making list after list with many revisions. We never stopped until we had every penny accounted for, even if it was crap on stick with glitter, it had to be under the tree come the 25th.

If my memory serves me right, we would then proceed to write Santa a letter, with a list of catalogue numbers, pages, prices, etc., included, never suspecting a thing. Now that I'm "grown-up", and knowing the financial hardships that my parents had to endure, it was a miracle we had Christmas at all. I think that "Santa Claus" needs to know how grateful Stephen, Judy and I am for giving us such wonderful Christmases in our home. I am sure that Santa has made many a visit to Pictou as well over the years, and should be thanked as well for his magic of making family memories that last forever.

Santa made his arrival to the City of Iqaluit last weekend

for the parade, and was all decked out in red as usual, but decided to wear tradition Inuit Kamiks and Caribou-fur trousers.
After the parade he took his throne in the community hall and
listened to the children, one after the other, tell him what they
want for Christmas. It was really a nice place to be that cold day
in December, watching child after child sit on Santa's Lap with
their gleaming or bashful smiles. For each child that Santa
entertained, a memory of Christmas at home entered my head.

So, first and foremost, Kelly and I would like to wish
Santa a very Merry Christmas, and to everyone in Pictou
County and Cape Breton, our warmest thoughts and best wish-
es for the holiday season.

Happy New Year

It should be no surprise that this weekend will see the end of 2004 and the arrival of 2005. This is a time when most people look back and reflect upon the year that has just past, and make resolutions for the up-coming one. So, I thought I would do just that this week.

The reason I started to write these columns was for a variety of reasons, but two main ones stick out in my mind. First, I wanted to remind people living in Pictou County, what they have to be proud about and how it could be worse. Secondly, I wanted to share the experience of living North of 60 from a Nova Scotian point of view, and pass on the many great things that I have learned since I arrived. Leaving a predominantly Scottish culture to reside in an Inuit/Arctic culture certainly had its ups and downs.

2004 was filled with many funny moments. Some I shared with you, dragging a dog home tied to the back of our truck; to enjoying a sled ride down the bay being hauled by eight flatulating huskies. Who could forget me popping the button off of my pants during lunch break, and stapling them back closed to avoid suspicion at work. That is just to mention but a few, and there were quite a few that I didn't. An I won't, because "you-know-who" doesn't know about them either. Ha ha

But with the good must come some bad, this year I lost a really close friend, one that I think about each and every week at some point. It also has seen the passing of one Pictou County's finest gals, Mrs. Gladys McCabe. Gladys was a much-loved mother to Barbara-Ann and her siblings, and a cherished grandmother to Kelly and many other grandchildren. The New Year will not be the same without them.

We have traveled close to the Arctic Circle when we

spent a weekend in Pangnirtung, spent time swimming with the dolphins in South Carolina, and visited the Shiretown on three different occasions. We spent days on end seeing daylight for only a brief period, and equally as many without the darkness to close the day. All and all, we had an adventure that will last a lifetime, one with few regrets, being away from family notwith-standing.

So, what are the plans for the New Year, resolutions you might ask? Well, I should work on getting rid of the keg around my waist and try to find a six pack to replace it. I should tell my wife that I love her more often but ultimately, my strongest resolve will be not to see the end of 2005 in the North, but rather share it in Nova Scotia with friends and family where I belong.

Happy New Year.

Brains and Trains

Now, let me tell you this. When the big guy was handing out brains, I must have heard trains and said, "No thanks, don't know how to use one, in consequence, don't need one or want one." While you good folks are enjoying pretty nice weather, we have been punished day after day with an average of -35C and that's without the wind-chill factored in.

The tow trucks are constantly hauling vehicles into their garages for nothing else but just to warm them up enough to start. Our little truck, for the lack of a better description, gave us the "ole middle finger" the other day, and stopped dead in its tracks, refusing to move another inch because of the cold. It REALLY is that cold.

But where this story takes an interesting turn, is two days later. I used to walk from the bank to the pharmacy after work, which is like walking from the Royal Bank in Pictou to the post office. Not a far walk, so I never consider it to be exercise. So this particular afternoon, I left the bank and was waiting for a taxi to show up. But as I stood there, I thought about how there was really no wind to speak of and how good it might feel to walk home, a 20-minute walk. After all, I really could use some form of exercise that doesn't involve the walk up the stairs to our apartment.

So off I went like a moron, whistling zippity-do-da as I went. The first thing I noticed is how my parka was starting to freeze up, then my ears started to burn with that familiar sting of frostbite. Now, you are probably wondering at this point, how could my ears possibly be getting frostbitten through a toque? Well, let me tell you how. Some people look normal and attractive in a toque, others look like criminals, and then there are the dorks. Sorry to break the news, but it is really a 1 in 3 gamble. Me, I look like the President of Dorkville when I wear one, so I never had one on. That is until I could take the burning no more.

As my journey continued up the hill, eventually my jacket literally froze stiff to the point that I could not bend the arms. My cheeks were hard as stones, my kneecaps were stiffening up, and my entire legs were burning now. (A sensible man would wear long underwear as a rule in the North but you already know what I was not wearing). At the end of my journey, I was that frozen I didn't dare sit down in fear that my bum would break off.

I could literally feel my body start to freeze up during that 20-minute walk home. Why did I not hail a cab when I got so cold? Because I felt it would be a waste of money to get a cab for such a short distance, after all I was just about there and I was exercising. So 24 hours later, my ears are swollen, my weight is the same and I haven't seen certain parts of my lower body that only males can relate to. I heard about exercising until you feel the burn or how it won't kill you to walk more. Yeah, it would and almost did. I am finished with exercise. Long live Mr. Grumbley! That what I call my stomach since it has became its own entity. Choo-Choo…

The Apprentice

Most of us are aware of the vastly popular television show of Donald Trump's, The Apprentice. The season finale was aired just before Christmas and the winner was a real no-brainer for everyone involved, except Donald for some reason. Watching the show, seeing what hoops they had to jump through to appease the ego of Mr. Trump and his entourage, got me to thinking what it would be like if they had filmed the program in the North.

Well for starters, it might be tough to find enough candidates to audition for the job. You see, it is the goal of everyone to land a job with the G.N. (Government of Nunavut), and not in the private sector. In addition to that, Donald's company would have to be more than 50% Inuit-owned if he was interested in supplying any service to the North, with a tendered bid. So that would put a damper on the show as well.

The attitude towards non-Inuit employers and employees in general is not good to begin with, as it is seen as taking away jobs from the Inuit. One example of this attitude was illustrated recently in the paper, in which an all Inuit owned co-operative group advertised for the position of manager of the group. The job posting stated that a bachelors degree in business management was "desirable" but not necessary. That posting has raised the dandruff on quite a few people. They stated that Inuit wouldn't bother to apply because the standard was being set too high, leaving only non-Inuit to apply. Some co-ops have even threatened to leave the group, unless the bachelor degree phrase is removed.

The board of directors for the co-op has gone on record to say that they thought long and hard before they put that in, and did so to encourage post-secondary education to their people. There are too many uneducated people in positions of management and they only wanted to put a catalyst in place to start the process of change. I could do nothing but shake my head. I would think that they would want a university-educated candidate to lead their co-operative into the future, but hey, that's just my opinion. Now back to The Apprentice.

The contestants would not be able to work on weekends, overtime or any holidays. They would take time off to go hunting, fishing or just out on the land because they believe it is necessary in order to maintain their old ways. "Sorry Mr. Trump, nobody showed up for the taping of the show today, they said maybe tomorrow, if the weather is not good for fishing, but if it is, too bad, then maybe the next day." True as I am sitting here, I have dealt with that attitude here. Donald's infamous hair would be pulled out in frustration, which may be an improvement.

Cape Breton should be thinking of running its own version called " The Pogey", where contestants are challenged each week on how to get Pogey from different situations. One week they will be laid off, next week they apply to go back to get a trade, and of course the much highlighted Pogey run to Ontario. Now that would not only be entertaining but also informative to the viewers.

The $500 Snowmobile

January is a tough month to endure in the North. The days are short and extremely cold, relentless and without mercy. The holidays are over, nothing really in sight to look forward to except a mid-winter break. So anything out of the "ordinary" is a welcome break.

Harry Pierce, a daily visitor to the bank, was telling me how a friend of his had their snowmobile go through the sea-ice down the bay. The only thing stopping it from plunging to a deep-water burial was the Kamatik (sled) that was attached. The same one that is now pointing at a 45-degree angle. The skidoo had to be left there, as the surrounding ice was too soft for a rescue operation. So now that the ice has hardened, the skidoo is trapped in the sea-ice with the Kamatik jetting into the air like a piece of obscure art, the kind that has to be explained to me, and after, would still leave me just as confused.

Harry didn't witness the event, but related how that either it was going to cost $500 to get the skidoo out, or how

$500 buys the skidoo on a first come, as is, where is, basis. All he could remember as his friend told him was the price of $500.

But he did explain that his friend couldn't find his way out of a one-door bedroom unless the door was open. I never asked but he must be related to Ole Crack Corn.

Now, that is a sight one isn't going to see everyday, so what would you have me do. Stay home and pontificate the laws that society tells us are just and true. Exactly, I was off down the bay the first chance I got to get a look at the Snowmobile Artwork, or rescue operation, and/or possible birthday gift for Kelly. Always thinking, I am.

The weather was cold as a mother in law's heart. Not mine, but other peoples, I adore mine, (how is that for sucking up) and the daylight was getting thin, but I forged my way down the bay for about an hour before turning back because of looming bad weather. I never did see the skidoo in question, but I did see a lot of ice and snow. In hindsight, I really should have thought the whole plan through better anyway. There are polar bears out on the ice now looking for seals, and they do that where the ice is not formed fully. Logically, if the skidoo went through the ice and is refreezing there as we speak; the nice, white, stalking, cuddly, predatory bears wouldn't be far.

That is one thing that you always have to be conscientious of when going out on the land. Polar bears will stalk a human being, and with my yellow helmet on, I would be like a big tasty M&M to the bears. Crunchy on the outside but sweet on the inside, and I wouldn't melt in his paws. A huge treat for them, I would think. Not necessarily for me though.

I will try again later but not until the ice is formed farther down the bay, and not without other riders because of the distance and fear of breakdowns. I will keep you posted on the venture, but will leave you with a hint for next week. If you like the Leafs, you might want to ignore this article, and please, please leave your bedroom door open. Ha ha ha. Burn....

Was it Really The Team or Not?

This is usually the time of year that hockey fans take the standings seriously and start to predict the Stanley Cup winner. This isn't happening this year as we all know, but Leaf fans, are taking it in stride, I believe because their team will finish as they always do, season or no season, without the Cup. I was talking to many of my Leaf fan friends, telling them how I really thought this could have been the year, ha ha ha. As I was teasing them, I began to ponder about other avenues to harass them, and then it came to me how some players have opted to play in other leagues until the dispute is settled. If these players could not win a championship as a collective, I got to wonder how the teams they are playing for now were fairing out.

Well, I did a minor amount of searching on the internet and came to an early, and maybe premature conclusion. I checked out the AHL, and they are not winning, and I checked out the Swedish Elite League and guess what? They are not winning either. So, although it is early, I will predict the championship drought for the Leafs will continue into 2006 at the very least. As you can see, another brilliant avenue of harassment for my friends; my poor, poor friends.

As a good friend, I should be trying to make them feel good about themselves and not continue to denounce their choices. So, I decided to let them in on some of the sadness we Hab fans have to deal with. By being a Hab fan, I can never know what it feels like to support a team that has not won the Stanley Cup in my entire life. I will never know what kind of dedication it must take to always remain so positive, year after losing year. But I am thankful for them being there to help me in understanding.

Friendship is only truly cherished when you share your strengths and weaknesses with those of your friends. Each taking away from each other what helps them to become a better-rounded person. As I look back at my closest friends, I can see exactly why we were friends, what we shared in common and what we secretly envied about each other.

Obviously, my Leaf Fans like me for my popularity and humility. He he, while I remain friends with them for their unyielding loyalty to the sinking ship called the Leafs. That should be enough punishment for them for the remaining year. Not another word on this subject until next year. And to show you that I truly do support you, GO Leafs GO!!!

The Return of the Sun

Last week had marked a momentous occasion for some people living in the North. As I mentioned early on, the Canadian Arctic has a tremendous difference in climate and environment compared to the rest of the country. For one thing, the days on Baffin Island swing from having approximately 4.5 hours of light around the 21 of December, to 4.5 hours of darkness six months later. If you live higher in the North, like Arctic Bay or Resolute Bay, you may never see the sun at all for months on end.

Although we never lose the sun completely in Iqaluit, most days you have only ambient and not direct sunshine as the sun is so low on the horizon. The city itself is mainly built in three tiers from the shore up, each higher than the other, with a fourth tier just being completed on the road-to-nowhere subdivision. If you live on the first level and if it is a clear day, you will be able to see the sun over the bay, but living on the third level like we do, we lose sight of the sun in November from our windows. Last week marked the return of the sun into the apartment as it finally went high enough in the sky to crest the third tier. It was a real sight for sore eyes. Further up island, there are celebrations marking the return of the sun, but they are still weeks away for them. I couldn't even imagine how they live in such conditions. As bad as the weather has been in Nova Scotia lately, and as cold and dark as it had been here (we had a wind-chill of -70C last Thursday) it is still better than what they are going through. It is always easy to complain about your situation, until you actually realize what others have to endure.

I know I will come off sounding really corny by saying what I am going to say. And if I was there I am certain I would be cursing the snow and the plow driver for blocking the driveway for what would seem to be the 12th time in one day. But after living here, and enduring the harsh Arctic winters, I would give anything to be home right now, waist or chest deep in snow. A friend of mine, Dave Waddell, is currently training in Victoria; B.C. having balmy albeit, wet 10 degree weather, but would trade it all to be in Pictou County with his family and friends. My best friend, Trevor Rorison, is also wishing for the comforts of Pictou County, but in a more indirect way. You see, he and his wife just moved from Oklahoma to Alabama, to a college town bordering Georgia. Now he works for a company that is about a half hour drive from his house, but because it is in Georgia, he has to cross the time zone to get to work. He has to get up an hour earlier just to get to work on time. That means usually 4:30 in the morning. At least in Nova Scotia, a half hour drive means exactly just that, thirty minutes.

So next time you think living in Pictou County sucks, just remember that it could always be worse, and there are enough people to tell you how. Take me for example; I have no trouble at all expressing how lucky Nova Scotians are to be living in Canada's best province.

Just Doesn't Make Sense, Really it Doesn't

I never once professed to be the brightest bulb in the house, and I realize that a lot of strange things are done in the world for good reasons. But the least these greater minds could do is explain why policies are as they are. A shining example is how the Government of Nunavut has repatriated its Liquor Management completely from the North West Territories. What does this mean exactly, you ask?

Well, since April 01, 1999, the date the Territory of Nunavut was established, access to the Yellowknife Liquor store in NWT was cut off. If anyone wanted to order alcohol they were required to obtain a permit from the Government of Nunavut to import it. There is a Liquor Warehouse located in Iqaluit, and has been for many years, but its function is to only serve the licensed establishments in the Territory, no walk-in purchases allowed.

With the repatriation just announced, with the intention of keeping revenues within the territory, they opened another warehouse in Rankin Inlet, where anybody can order their libations without a permit, as long as their respective community allows it. Within the Territory, there are five non-restricted communities, 12 restricted (liquor is allowed but one has to get the order approved by their local alcohol education committee, frivolous orders have the same chance of getting approval as the Eagles do of winning the Super Bowl) and eight dry communities. But the kicker is, still no walk in traffic. A person living in Iqaluit can order and buy alcohol without a permit from the Rankin Warehouse and vice versa. Bear in mind also, that if the Rankin branch doesn't have what you ordered in stock, it would be shipped to Rankin from Iqaluit, only to be shipped back to Iqaluit for delivery. Now you tell me, I am just plain stupid or does that not make any sense? Both communities are not restricted and anyone can order as much as they want and as often as they please, as long as it is from the other warehouse.

That would be like residents of New Glasgow walking into the NSLC, and being told you can place any order you want but from Pictou only, and have it shipped to you, however if they are out of stock, they will have to ship it to them so they can ship it to you. So it may take a couple of days. All the while, knowing full well, that right behind him is what you want. You have to pay for the product, a shipping and handling fee and the airfreight costs associated.

Not that this whole tied-selling racket affects me, but how can officials within the department justify this policy without looking silly. But like I said, there are greater minds at work in this place than mine. So until next week, take care of each other and we will see you all in March.

A Whole New World

Groundhog Day has come and gone, and the prognosticating rodents may or may not have announced six more weeks of winter, depending on whether you listened to Sam, Phil, or the other guy. Being above the 60th parallel, the general consensus is six more months of winter regardless of what any hog has to say. But either way, time marches on and summer will arrive eventually, even up here.

This summer will see a great deal of change in our lives again. For starters, we will be making the move back home, the Arctic adventure chapter in the story of our lives concluded. But the most exciting part of the arrival of summer 2005 will be the birth our first child. We are really excited about the news. When we told our families, they reacted with a lot of crying and tears. Hmmmm, looking back, I am not sure that was the reaction I was looking for, but, I remember Ira crying like a baby when I proposed to Kelly. So, they were all tears of joy I'm sure. He he.

The thing I have noticed though, is how many manuals, books and magazines there are for women and pregnancy, but nothing for men. Before I get inundated with a barrage of titles, remember that I am in the North, with no Chapters or Coles bookstores. So my search has been quite limited, but I would think though that after centuries of written prose some guy would have documented the event from a mans perspective, you know like a hand-to-hand combat instructional manual.

I have come to understand that with pregnancy, comes added responsibilities, such as cleaning cat litter for nine months, or more, for health reasons, lifting heavy objects, going to the store for crazy food cravings (none yet, but I am waiting for it). However, since the joyful day I found out, all the relationship rules have changed again. There is no wonder men can't understand women. There's one set of rules for meeting them another set for dating. Once we figure what they are, and we have a successful relationship, Bang, you're engaged and trying to figure out the new rules. I was fortunate though, Kelly told me early in the engagement that she was in charge and would tell me what to do, so basically I just kept my mouth closed, had a wonderful wedding day, then slipped into marriage, with different rules again. Now the rules have changed again, and from what I read in Kelly's manuals and books on the subject, hormones are going to start flying and I better be prepared for a whole new world to experience. I wish there was a groundhog that could predict what a woman's next thought or emotion would be instead of the weather. Now that would be worth watching once a year, even in the North.

The Qulliq

When most people picture the Arctic, images are conjured up of igloos, polar bears, and Inuit with fur-rimmed faces. However there are many other images that are uniquely Northern that don't seem to appear in the mind's eye. There is the Ulu, a half-moon shaped knife used to cut and scrape the meat off of an animals hide, a traditional Inuit drum which is about a meter in diameter and 5 centimeters wide, looking like a huge ping-pong paddle, or today's topic, the qulliq or Inuit lamp.

The qulliq are carved out of stone, consisting of a shallow, slanted base shaped like a half circle to hold the fuel. Along the straight edge is where the wick is placed. A beater or stick is necessary to work the fuel and wick to permit an elongated row of fire. The unique design and construction of the Qulliq (lamp) allowed for production of both heat and light, as well as being compact enough to make transporting easy.

Fuel for the qulliq was harvested seal or narwhal fat for

coastal Inuit, and caribou fat for inland Inuit. The wicks were traditionally made from Arctic cotton, but threads from flour bags made excellent substitutions later on. Lighting and trimming of the qulliq was, and still is, an art and generally the responsibility of the women.

With short days of winter allowing little if any light at all, the lamps were an essential part of the Inuit survival. If the seal hunt were going bad, then the Qulliq would not have enough fat to light, which had devastating results. There would be no heat for the Igloo, no fire to boil water and food, no light for making or mending clothing and fixing hunting equipment. The days were so short that every moment of daylight had to be utilized in the hunt and without properly-working hunting/fishing equipment, well you get the picture, the cycle just continues.

A properly lit and trimmed qulliq also would serve as a beacon to the hunters as the Igloo's would glow on the nights horizon, helping them find their way home. Some elders would say that the dogs would see the light and instantly get their second wind, quickly and eagerly picking up the pace.

So as you can see, the qulliq was an extremely important fixture for the Inuit and their ultimate survival. With tourism being such a big part of Pictou Counties' survival, maybe we can all look for something as significant to our culture as the qulliq was to the Inuit and successfully market it. The light at the end of the tunnel sort of.

How to Live Longer

While I was at work the other day, I believe I might have stumbled across the secret to living longer. It was right under my nose all these years; I just never put two and two together, until now.

Time is really an interesting concept when one stops and thinks about it. There are days that fly by and days that drag on and on. When you are having a good time, there is never enough time, but when you are waiting in the line for the bathroom, you can actually see the hair grow longer on the person standing in front of you.

The other day at work was one of those days, and don't be fooled by the expression that time will fly right by when you are busy. You would think so but it is never a guarantee. The day started off busy and stayed that way all day. I'm sure we celebrated Valentines and Easter that day.

So I started to ponder during my seemingly, extremely short break, what if I did everything that dragged time? I could live to be older than Methuselah's Goat. Logically, I would have to put my theory to the test first, so I would have to compile a list of activities that stretch time like an elastic band.

Well, and before you laugh, I tried it in the past. Exercise. I had a membership at the YMCA in Pictou and planned on turning this dump truck of a body into a hot, sexy, sports car. I was to start off with a walk on the treadmill to warm-up fifteen minutes was the recommended time. That, my friends always seemed more like an hour than 15 minutes. (On a side note, I had to enter my age, weight, and other info into the machine to get it started. If anyone was on the other machines, I protected that info better than my PIN numbers for debit machines, so much so, that I have seen myself subtract years from my life and immediately lost 15 lbs just punching the data in.) An hour workout always seemed like an eternity and what was left of my self-esteem shattered. I would use a machine, usually with no weights attached, because I was either lazy or weak, but would add manly weight to them when I cleaned the machine for the next user. They must have been impressed at my strength.

Waiting; in lineups, doctor's offices, hospitals, or for elevators, is all good for lengthening your life, as would be watching documentaries on the migrating patterns of flocking Asian birds or listening to really bad singers. I could effectively double time if I do any of the above during the last 30 minutes of the workday, kind of like a Daily Double.

Some proof to support this theory might lie in my general observation that old people spend a lot of time in and around medical facilities, elevators (because the stairs are no longer an option), and watching nature documentaries and everyone knows that the average age of humans is getting longer and longer every year.

So that's my plan, if I start now I should be writing for a long, long, long time. I know, I know, you are thinking, lucky us.

Winter Driving

With only a few kilometers of roads to drive on in any community in the north, you would think that the perils of winter driving would be next to nil. I soon learned that nothing changes except for the speed.

The city of Iqaluit has few paved roads, three to be exact, and the rest are all dirt. The winter actually makes the roads smoother to drive on because all the potholes are filled with packed snow and ice, but that also means that they are extremely slippery.

Blizzards are always a concern for drivers because when one hits, visibility drops to nothing and I mean nothing. They put up a series of green and orange reflective poles along the main road, green for the right side and orange for the wrong side. So when the visibility drops when you are driving you can rely on the colour coded poles to make sure you don't go off the road. The only flaw in the system is that you have to be able to see them.

I had the pleasure of driving in one this winter and it was horrible. I was playing in the pit band for the high school musical on a Saturday night, and a blizzard started during the first act. What would normally take me less than 5 minutes to drive took me 30 minutes. I literally had to stop every few feet and get out to search for the road. Ok, move to the right dummy; get out, too far, move left, and so on until I reached home.

I realize that I could have done it a lot faster if I had someone with me. I seem to have become accustom to the spirit of a co-operative and teamwork approach to winter driving. In my younger days, I would spent many weekends driving from North Sydney to Sackville, NB, with my mother in tow, to visit my brother and sister at Mount A. Every time a car ahead of us would fishtail or slide, she would gasp, grab my arm, and tell me to watch out. Let us not forget the "uhhhh" starting quietly and getting louder while white knuckling the door handle and dash. Being married and living in the north hasn't stopped this team method any. I am constantly reminded, as I drive the 30km/hr speed limit, to watch out, that the roads are slippery, and the classic scream to "Look out!!" This advice always makes any drivers heart jump. Did they see something that we didn't? Is there some impending doom lying ahead that only they can foretell? Of course not, they are facing the same way we are, watching the same road, but it is that relationship that delivers a certain comfort zone for drivers and makes winter driving as safe as it is. I think a study should be done on winter driving mishaps and see if lone drivers have them more frequently than tag-team vehicle operators. I believe that the results would be eye popping.

So in the interim, for all you lone drivers, get out there, find that special someone and re-create the pleasure of winter driving that is oh so familiar to many drivers. You all know who you are.

Vegas Vacation

I think everyone has dreamt of going to Las Vegas, winning it big and turning a few meager dollars into a retirement plan. There are plenty of movies and television shows that show exactly that. But few people actually make the trip and even fewer find their retirement package. The hard part is not the actual winning of money, but the retention of your winnings, as it turns out.

Our vacation started out in an overstuffed airport. Three days of blizzards stopped air travel, and well, everything else in the North as far as that goes. When the storm finally ended, there were three days of flights to catch up on, so we knew without saying, that the plane would be stuffed. A three-hour flight in a jam-packed plane, didn't dampen our spirits one bit. That was until the smell of a rotting pile of festering, sweating flesh filled the cabin.

Now I have to be brutally honest with a few of you. If at any point in your life, you were told that your feet stink, or if you had to wash your feet because you were finding the smell a wee bit overpowering; then you should NEVER TAKE YOUR SHOES OFF ON A PLANE to let your puppies have some air. Hahaha, seriously though, give it a little thought. I believe they burned the plane after we got off.

Barring the smell, and losing our luggage for eight hours, the trip was off to a great start. We were excited about the sights and sounds of the strip, and the warmth of course.

I actually did very little gambling, as neither one of us were that interested, but did manage to win over $300 only to end up spending it in Vegas anyway. Not on gambling , but for food, shopping, hair products, etc, etc. And the hotels/casinos count on that. With big names like Rolex, Gucci, Prada, and all the other top names in fashion located within the Casinos themselves, money doesn't stay in your wallet long. Public school was good enough for me and it will be good enough for our children as well.

We did get out to see some shows while we were there. None of the big names like Celine Dion, Ray Romano, or Jay Leno, not that we didn't want to, but because there was just too many other things to do and see. The city seems to go all night, but all the shows are during the 7pm-12 pm slot. So unless you spend a month there, you will never see them all. The Penn and Teller show was easy for us to cross off our list. Their show was billed as the only show in Vegas with knives, guns, fire, one gorilla and a showgirl. I told Kelly, "Oh no, we have been to weddings in Antigonish before, including Terry Gottschall's. There would be nothing new to see at that show." Ha ha ha

The long and short of it all is this, Las Vegas is like Disney for adults. Extravance is abundant, money is everywhere, the food is great, and excitement fills the air. It is not the place to gain your financial security, but it might be the right spot to lose your shirt, and hopefully not your shoes for those reasons aforementioned. (Big word, he he)

Skijoring

I think most of us are familiar with the standard fare in winter sports. There's hockey, if we are lucky (but I promised not to talk about that for awhile), skiing, curling, figure skating and a host more to fill an Olympic arena. In recent years, extreme sports and variations on old favorites are popping up everywhere.

One such "hybrid" sport that's growing in popularity here and elsewhere is skijoring. If this is a new term to you, it's a sport developed from cross-county skiing and dog sledding. Are you getting the picture? Yeah, that's right, you strap on your cross-country skis, put a harness around your body, harnesses on your dogs and join everything with a bungee cord. After you are attached to your sled dogs, you encourage them to run real fast. Not for the faint of heart, or weak in the legs, kind of person.

Occasionally, I see these brave/foolhardy souls out on the bay with their dogs and can't help but think of how the sport would translate to Pictou. As I close my eyes, I can envision Helen Grant racing down the Jitney trail with Barney, her standard poodle, being trailed closely by Sherri-Lee Walsh with her lab. Another ambitious rider, as I'm sure all of her friends could attest to, would be Barbara-Ann as she has dreamed for years of dog sledding with her Keeshonds. Keeshonds have the look of northern dogs with their long fur and curly tails but were originally bred in the Netherlands, so dogsledding wouldn't be a natural instinct. Another thing that her friends can attest to is how her dogs don't really possess the necessary skills for dog sledding.

Now some of you will say, "But Robbie, you're a beagle person. Aren't you just biased?" Well, yeah, but Kelly can back me up on this one. Years ago, she used to take the dogs with her cross-country skiing. Not strapped to her, but for exercise and company. Five minutes into the run, both of them would try to sit on the back of the skis for a free ride!! Too bad Barbara-Ann, I guess dogsledding and skijoring for that matter are out of the question for you and your dogs. Maybe you should get some beagles.

On a related note, we went for a skidoo ride out on the bay on the weekend and were met by yet another unusual sight on the way back. I thought my eyes were deceiving me but no, I was witnessing the birth of another new hybrid sport. A man on skis was being towed across the bay by a snowmobile, with two more waiting for their turns. I haven't heard the name of this new-fangled sport, maybe ski-dooing, no wait that's already taken. 'Oh wait, I have it - blessed stupidity, - can't wait to try it.

Soundtracks

Let's face it; a movie would not be a movie without the soundtrack. I once read that a good soundtrack should be able to stand on its own musically, independent of the film, and should be more of a concert of emotions than a collection of different songs. From the opening trailers to the rolling credits at the end, a soundtrack will tell us how we should be feeling at any given moment. Here is where I believe I solved another one of life's little mysteries.

I believe that soundtracks are why some women think that their men are sensitive. Take me for example, I have found myself filled with tears while watching "Fried Green Tomatoes" or "Steel Magnolias" but when I find myself encountering similar scenarios in real life, I never feel that way. Why? No music.

When couples first start to date, movies are a big part of the experience, hence women see men showing their "sensitive" side early in the game. Later in the relationship, when faced with a real life dilemma, and showing no emotion, they comment on how strong he was. "A real rock" is what they would tell their friends afterwards. In reality, he probably would have been wiping his running nose on his sleeves if there had been appropriate music playing in the background, but since there wasn't, dry eyes.

I am not saying that every guy is like this, but I believe the majority of men are. I am certain that there are men out there that look for the Kleenex when the petals fall off of a rose bloom or get all out of sorts when their friends split up, but they are in the minority.

Now that Kelly is expecting and her hormones are going crazy; something that will correct itself after the birth I hope, ha ha, she has found herself crying at simple things and for no reason whatsoever. From the onset of the pregnancy, there didn't seem to be one really definitive moment to confirm her condition in her mind. That was until she wept during a girly movie. The movie itself was not emotional driven enough to make a normal person cry, but couple it with a soundtrack and raging hormones, wham-bam, tears.

So in the end, life would be truly more emotional if there was a sound track playing in the background, but until that happens, I guess the guys will just have to remain strong.

Three years later!

The Visit

Well, even I have to admit when I have it good, and for the last two years, I've had it pretty good in one respect. For a married guy, I never have to worry about my in-laws popping in unexpected. Don't get me wrong, I love Ira and Barbara-Ann, and always look forward to spending time with them, but I also know that some married men would love to be in my position.

Last summer, my family (Kelly's in-laws) journeyed to Iqaluit for a visit and this week will see the arrival of Barbara-Ann to the Great White North.  Ira was here years ago working with the fishermen, and is not making the trip, he opted to stay home and look after the home fires. Barbara-Ann's trip was planned to correspond with the Toonik Tyme Festival. I only hope the North is ready for her and vice-versa, because we have a big week planned for her.

On the day she arrives, we will greet her at the airport and settle her in. Later that day, we will be taking her to a community feast for supper. This is where she will be able to dine on traditional northern or country food. There will be lots of raw seal, Muktuq (whale blubber) and frozen and raw Caribou to chew on. I figure if we start her off that way, she won't complain about my cooking the rest of her visit.

Monday evening is the opening ceremonies, with lots of music, throat singing and drum dancing. It is also the time when they will draw the lucky contestants for this year's Fear Factor. Everyone who wants to take part enters their name and then six names will be drawn. And before you ask, no I am not taking part, but Barbara-Ann may be lucky enough, I entered her in the running. Well, when else will she get the chance to go toe to toe with Ole Jimmy Cracked Corn in a Caribou eyeball-eating contest? Ha ha ha, good times my friends, good times.

The rest of the week will be filled with a northern fashion show, scavenger hunt, museum visiting and craft fairs. I have a skidoo lined up for her, so we can spend the day out on the land and sea-ice exploring the beauty of the North. Now I realize that certain Inuit legends might reflect that it was customary to put the elderly on an ice-flow to meet their maker when they outlive their usefulness . Let me assure you, I don't think she is elderly or useless and have nothing but good intentions on returning her to Pictou safe and sound. After all, I will need free baby-sitting services soon.

So all in all, a big week is in store for her. Honestly, it will be nice to see her and really nice that she will be able to see, taste and hear everything that makes for a true northern experience. So if anyone needs any fermented walrus meat, known as Iqunaq, let her know, she probably won't charge you too much for the shipping.

Crime and Punishment

Crime in Iqaluit is considerably higher than it is in Pictou County. The local division of the RCMP is going non-stop. We have a constable living in our building and he has quite a few horror stories under his belt.

The majority of the crime is domestic violence, although we have had a number of murders in the last couple of years as well. Theft and vandalism account for the remainder of incidents. When I worked at the Quickie-Mart, shoplifting was a common occurrence, but few if any make it through the justice system because of the limited number of legal professionals, resources and time.

With such a high turnover of staff in retail stores, the chance of the employee still working for the company, or still living in the North for that matter, is slim to none, if and when a court date arrives. The justice system just doesn't have the money to fly witnesses back for the trials. The common practice is to get a banning order from the store, forbidding the culprit from entering the premises for an established amount of time. But again, with a high staff turnover, it doesn't take that long for the shoplifter to freely enter the store again with no fear. So the opportunity for the circle of crime to continue is always there

The Baffin Correctional Center (BCC) is the territorial detention facility, and runs a little different than our provincial jails. Inmates are housed from all over the territory, excluding the violent offenders; who are sent to Ontario to a more secure facility. The inmates in BCC are involved in a system of restorative justice. They spend time out on the land with elders, learning the traditional way of Inuit life. They have a softball team that is part of the Iqaluit Softball League, and they frequently take part in 4 on 4 basketball tournaments in order not to isolate them from society completely, making the transition back smoother.

There are really too many issues at play here for me to accurately pass judgment on how the system works. However, I think that if the elders in the community are taking the time to help the youth find their way, it seems like a step in the right direction to me.

For those of you who may have concerns about "poor" Barbara-Ann, she arrived safe and sound, and has already been out on the sea-ice without incident. She did hold on tighter than usual in fear of the ice flow story though. She wants everyone to know that she is having a wonderful time and loves all the skidooing. Poor Drew at home with no snow.

Earth Day

On Friday, the 23rd of April, a very special event took place in Iqaluit. In an effort to raise awareness about global warming, famed Los Angeles artist John Quigley was in town to create a project that would be sent around the world to coincide with Earth Day.

The project was to create a giant Inuit Drum Dancer with the words "Arctic" and "Warning" in English and "Listen" in Inuktitut. The creation was made out of roughly 700 people formed on the sea-ice and the picture taken from a helicopter above.

The weather was not really agreeable being around -32 C with the winds, and some people succumbed to the cold. Fortunately, for him he had some Hollywood star power to keep the remaining waiting to complete the picture.

Film stars Salma Hayek, known for her roles in "Frida" and "Desperado", and Jake Gyllenhaal, who played Dennis Quaid's son in the film "The Day After Tomorrow" were on hand to take part in the activity. And of course, n o t w i t h s t a n d i n g , Barbara-Ann and myself.

The picture was supposed to be taken at 1 pm but because of the winds, delays were inevitable, but at around 3 pm, we all headed out from the mustering area, like lemmings jumping off a cliff and sliding down in our bottoms to the sea-ice below. Once out there we were placed in position and the picture was taken.

The irony of the situation was as we were taking a stand against global warming, we had Barbara-Ann sitting and laying on the ice, melting it. Her words not mine.

After the picture was taken, we all had to make our way back to the top of the hill, a rigorous climb that almost did me in. But not our crafty Pictonian, no, not at all, she was too smart for that. The whole time she was laying on the ice, she was plotting on how to get back. Picture taken, she made her way over to a group of spectators and made her pitch, which had her pass me up the hill riding on the back of a strangers' Skidoo. Well done, I could have done the same I suppose, but thought that a near death experience, with almost having a stroke would, be good for me.

Did we get to meet the stars, you ask? Well, we took their picture on the ice, but that was as far as we got. Until we got back to the apartment that is. After we arrived home, I went back out to lock the skidoo up in front of the Quickie Mart next door, when who should stop to get some snacks but Salma and Jake.

I chatted briefly with them as they got out to go in the store but had no camera, no paper and no pen for autographs or photos. I bet Barbara Ann would have been more prepared. She probably would have faked an injury to get them to carry her up the stairs to the apartment in order to avoid climbing yet again and to get her autographs.

Barbara-Ann of Tumbledown Mountain

After two years in the North, I finally took part in an age-old tradition having tea out on the land. I cheated quite alot on the methodology, but the end result was basically the same, I believe.

During Barbara-Ann'visit, I took off from the bank at lunchtime one day, and took her out on the land. I borrowed a snow machine from friends for Barbara-Ann, and we headed out on the sea-ice and down the bay to Tarr Inlet, where we headed back onto land and deep into the frozen tundra.

In days of old, Inuit used to trek out to the Glaciers to chip ice, which they would take back, boil over their Qulliq's and brew their tea. This process would take a long time, hours really, but they claim that the inner ice of the glaciers is formed of "Old Water" and is the purest, best tasting water in the world for tea. The practice of getting glacial ice to make tea is still practiced in the north, but it is not that common anymore. I, on the other hand, filled the electric kettle with tap water, boiled it, and brewed the tea in the coffee pot before transferring it to the very non-Inuit, non-traditional Thermos.

After driving for about an hour and half, stopping periodically to muse or take pictures, Barbara-Ann said, "I hope you know how to get back", to which I replied, "I thought you were taking notes on how to get back." She was not amused. Traveling by Skidoo is easy as long as you stay on the trails that are there. If you veer off them you can get lost in a hurry. The day we went was not ideal as parts of the trail was blown over with snow, so we only went as far I remembered, had our much welcomed hot tea and headed back. Better to explore uncharted territory on a clear day.

Once back in Iqaluit we headed up to the radar station at upper base. Again, that trail was blown in and snowdrifts were quite challenging to maneuver. The funny thing was, that all day, I had her traverse rough sea-ice, boon dock on frozen riverbeds, and climb some hills that would frighten most amateur riders. All without incident and with what looked like the ease of a pro rider. That was until we got to the top and had to turn around. For some reason, as she was turning, she gunned it. Her right ski hit the bank as she was turning and instead of leaning up into the turn to balance the Skidoo, she leaned the way the Skidoo was and rolled off. At this time I was quite concerned that she hurt herself, but it was quite funny afterwards. When she rolled off the Skidoo, she never changed her body position at all. I only saw her for a second on the ground like an upside down turtle, as I had to stop her Skidoo from going down the hill by itself. I'm sure she was still giving the throttle the gas as she was laying there on her back. If I had picked her up and placed her back on the Skidoo, she would be in riding position. I now refer to her as Barbara-Ann of Tumbledown Mountain in honour of the event. Maybe Nunavut will market her like PEI did Anne of Green Gables.

The Plan

Spring is in the air in Pictou County, from what I hear, but, the same is not so here. The snow is still flying, and there lots of ice, wind and cold. The only sign that spring is just around the corner is the state of the roads. Finally ice and snow free, after a long time being covered, roads now come with potholes and wash boarding. I'm glad I don't have false teeth, because I am sure they would either shatter in my mouth or rattle out and fall on the floor just driving down the road.

This spring will mark the end of the northern adventure for us. Two years ago when we moved here, we had a two-year plan. The plan was stay for two years, and move home. Whenever you meet anyone living in the North, who is not from there originally, they all have a plan. Some are on a two-year plan as well, while others have a five-or ten-year plans.

Many people who arrive with a two-year plan, and end up spending many more. They end up staying for a variety of reasons, the lure of the money, the tax breaks, or maybe they ended up in a relationship while here. Regardless of the reasons, I haven't met anyone yet who stayed for the climate or the lifestyle.

Kelly, as some already know, is back at home and adjusting to being a "Southerner" again. I would have loved to arrive with her, but I had committed to quite a few events that I wouldn't feel right about abandoning. But come the 29th, I will be the first one on the plane, and you can mark your celestial calendars now, because I am predicting a full moon over Iqaluit that afternoon. Ha ha.

With three weeks to go, I have a lot of loose ends to tie up. I will perform these menial tasks with a great deal of enthusiasm, having the end well within my sights. I am really looking forward to the challenges of parenthood this summer, rekindling old relationships with friends and lets not forget, finding meaningful employment.

So if anyone knows where a former QuickieMart Squishie Master turned teller can find such employment, please don't let Kelly know.

My new plan is to get as much sun and heat this summer, as possible but I can only assume that she has other plans. Oh well, whatever happens, it will happen in Nova Scotia and that's fine by me.

We are embarking on a new plan.
The Pictou Plan

Community Games

I have always enjoyed games that involve the community. I believe they are designed in part to foster love, harmony, and togetherness within that community. There are standard games that seem to be perennial, the ones that never seem to fade in popularity. However, every so many years, a different game seems to take hold.

Trivial Pursuit was big once, as were a host of other trivia games. Charades and games where you were required to draw things also had their heyday. Now it seems that a version of poker has taken Pictou County by storm. The game you ask? Texas Hold 'Em.

Texas Hold 'Em card parties are becoming the new "in" thing to do in Pictou County. When I talk to friends at home, they all are playing, and on my last visit, I was at one of these parties. A bunch of us all meet at Duncan's and played into the night. The stakes that evening weren't high, but the players all thought they were and came to play big. The funny part was, the big winner wasn't the one who played big; it was the one who seemed to nonchalantly play the hands as she tended to her guests. I assume that she was using her duties as a host to keep us all from figuring out her poker face. The only other plausible explanation would be that she is actually better than Ira, Duncan and the rest of us. Nah, it has to be the poker face thing.

Now, up North, things seem to evolve at a different pace. There are no 45 games or cribbage, so the chance of finding a Texas Hold 'Em gathering would be slim. I was talking to numerous people and most never even heard of it. There were a few that have watched it on television but that's about all. Darts, TV Bingo and Karaoke are the events that have everyone involved.

Darts were never my thing, and if history has taught me anything at all, I shouldn't be singing in public under any circumstances. As far as playing bingo, I was once referred to as a bingo idiot. I went to a bingo hall in North Sydney with a co-worker who was, as it turned out, a professional player. I had one card to her eight. When B-8 was called, there would be a flurry of dabbers everywhere. I think I was splashed once. And there was me, tongue sticking out of the side of my mouth frantically searching before the next number was called.

At the end, I was just sitting there, drinking my pop and eating my chips, while she played my card as well. She was not very nice with her chitchat either. I had merely commented on her lovely collection of lucky trolls as she was in full swing of dabbing. That's when she called me an idiot and banned me from ever going with her again.

And to think that I thought community games were meant to foster brotherly love and togetherness.

Recycling Reality

Recycling is an important part of our lives in Pictou County. It is helping reduce the damage being done to our environment and making our part of the province a healthier and better place to live. Growing up in Cape Breton, we never recycled at all. The first sign of change that I can remember is when the Pop-Shop came to town. We used to go get two or three cases of pop, then bring the bottles back for return or exchange.

When I made the move from the Island to Pictou, I was in for a big change in lifestyle. No longer could I use one black bag for everything. I hated it at the start, but as time went on, I started to become accustomed to the daily routine. Lectures from Kelly about what does, and doesn't, go in each bag were always there to remind me. Kelly's cousin Lesley was living there as well, so we used to subconsciously use each other to take the blame for misusing the program. It got so bad, at one point that she went to the effort and trouble to sit Lesley and me down and quiz us on recycling etiquette.

The move to the North brought us back to a recycling free area again, one bag for everything. In all fairness, they are trying recycling options on a basic level, but the costs of recycling in the north are extremely high and not recycling saves the city much needed money to run its other essential services. It is a real conundrum, a recycling program reduces essential services and much needed social services making the city vulnerable, while not recycling helps the city meet its demands but puts the environment at risk.

Since Kelly has been home, she is getting back in the recycling groove, but not without its setbacks. What goes where, and what doesn't go where. Not having been able to practice her craft the last two years, she actually had to call the Recycling Hotline to find out where milk cartons go. I only wish that Lesley and I were there to witness the call.

My return to the land of the trees and grass next week will also mark the return of daily lectures about not putting Tim Horton's cups in the green bin with the plastic lids still on, or stop putting the paper with plastic. Oh well, I survived it once, I will again. Diapers will be a challenge I m sure, but I`m not worried, we agreed that she would change all of them, while I do the entire knee bouncing. Ha ha.

From Iqaluit to Pictou

Two years ago, Kelly and I moved from our Shire town to the capital of Canada's newest territory to start a new chapter and adventure in our lives. During that time, we experienced some really neat things. Coming from our Down East culture and immersing ourselves into a Northern culture meant, for probably the first time in our lives, living as a visible minority. However there were no regrets, quite a few memorable moments, and one real valuable lesson learned.

I will not miss the weather, isolation, or endless hours of daylight and darkness. It will be the people I will miss most of all. I had the extreme pleasure of meeting and working alongside some of the best people I have ever known.

The cadets and staff of 795 Royal Canadian Air Cadet Squadron welcomed us both with open arms and hospitality. These young cadets had shown me the very best that their people and culture had to offer. I had never worked with a better Squadron and they should be very proud of themselves for that because I have worked with thousand of cadets over the years.

I am also really going miss the security of constant employment that the north has to offer. First, working at the QuickStop alongside Ole Jimmy Crack Corn made for quite a few frustrations but more laughs and in the end I will look back and wish him well.

Secondly, the people at the Royal Bank, they were the very best. I have worked a lot of different jobs in my life and never minded any of them; work was exactly that to me, work. It wasn't meant to be fun. But working here was fun and enjoyable. The staff has a high turnover rate compared to the Maritimes, 9 out of 13 employees had moved on in the year I was there alone, me included. I wish I could move the whole branch, building, staff and all to Pictou and continue the relationship. I will miss them, but not enough to stay. They are welcome to visit any time, as our house is always open.

Nope, I am really happy to be getting back home to my own culture, my own family, and my close friends. There is no better place, in my opinion, to settle and raise a family than in our great province, both of which I will be doing. I have learned much and have shared much in the past couple of years, but the most important lesson we both learned was, what good is making and having money if you don't have your close friends and family around to share it with.

The Final Chapter

Now that my northern adventure is finally over, I can get back to reality in Nova Scotia. I have been back for a week now and it is starting to feel like home again. I have lots of things to do around the house before I can really start to enjoy the summer. Kelly has made sure that my hands will not be idle for a long time.

Everyone has made me feel so welcome to be back, even complete strangers. I was applying for MSI last week and the lady I was talking to welcomed me back home, a small gesture but it really said it all, I was really home.

Between coats of paint and assembling some of the many pieces of furniture that Kelly bought, I had time to re-explore my surroundings and see what's new in Pictou. There are a lot of new and improved buildings and certainly new businesses since I left. All signs that show Pictou is moving ahead and trying to maintain its status as the great Shiretown of the Province.

This will be my last time writing The Real Northern News seeing how I am not in the real north anymore. It was really a pleasure to have shared our north-of-60 experiences with you all. Writing each week helped us keep in touch with our roots, it was a project that took us out of the Arctic and put us back in Pictou once a week, at least in our minds and thoughts. You have shared a lot of my laughter, fascination of a different way of life, and occasional moments of sadness. I have shared just as much about Pictou County in Iqaluit as I have shared with you here about the North. I have encouraged everybody I knew to stop by and visit whenever they get the chance. A few have already and have had nothing but nice things to say.

Next week, I hope to start with a fresh new title that

reflects the change in location. I am not sure yet what it will be yet, "Ramblings from an Idiot" has a nice ring to it, ha ha, but we will all have to wait to see. I hope to keep the format the same as it is now, and have a number of ideas already to talk about, such as my Pit-a-poo project and the time I saved Ira from having to prepare and serve dinner for two at a charity auction.

So I will end our Real Northern News experience here by saying goodbye and thank you in Inuktitut.

Tavvauvutit and Nakurmiik!

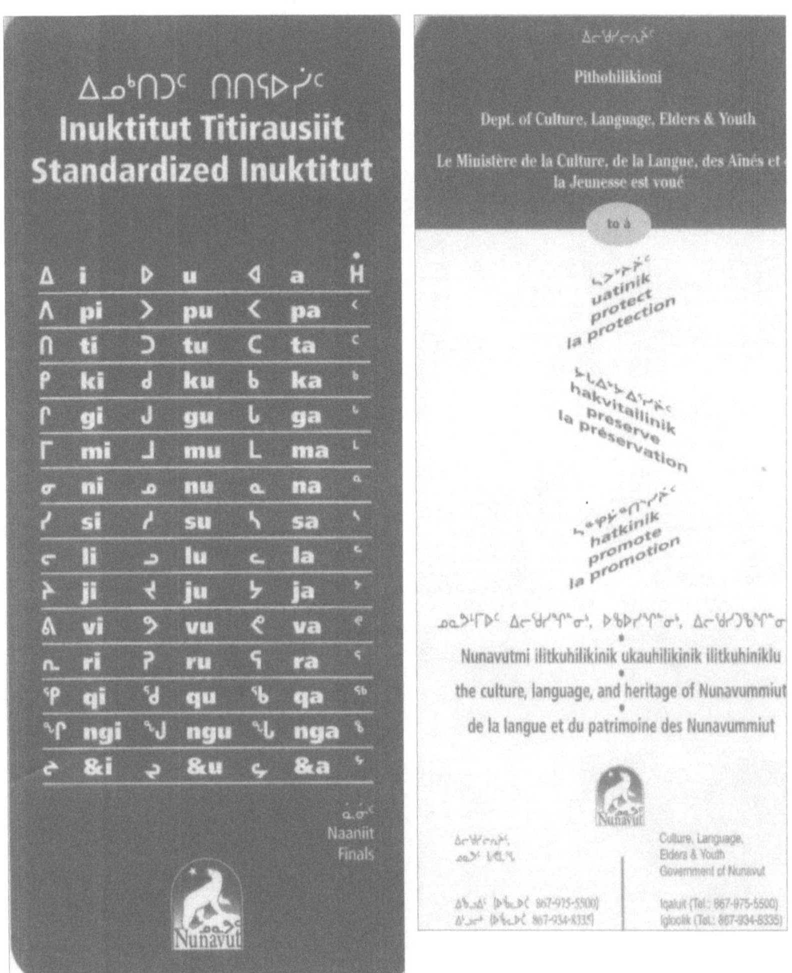

The gouvernment of Nunavut, Dept. of Culture, Language & Heritage Elders & Youth, provide these cards to help preserve and promote local language.